PERSPECTIVES ON EARLY CHILDHOOD PSYCHOLOGY AND EDUCATION

SPECIAL FOCUS

Parenting and Young Children

Volume 1, Issue 1
Spring 2016

Copyright © 2016
Pace University Press
41 Park Row
15th floor
New York, NY 10038

ISBN: 978-0-9619518-6-3
ISSN: 2471-1527

Member

Council of Editors of Learned Journals

Special thanks to Jaleh Davari
Gonzaga University Graduate Assistant

PERSPECTIVES on EARLY CHILDHOOD PSYCHOLOGY and EDUCATION

EDITOR
Vincent C. Alfonso, *Gonzaga University*

SPECIAL FOCUS EDITORS
Barbara A. Mowder and Renee Krochek

EDITORIAL REVIEW BOARD
Vincent C. Alfonso, *Gonzaga University*
Stephen Bagnato, *University of Pittsburgh*
Renee Bergeron, *Consultant*
Zeynep Biringen, *Colorado State University*
Bruce Bracken, *College of William & Mary*
Melissa Bray, *University of Connecticut*
Victoria Comerchero, *Touro College*
Gerard Costa, *Montclair University*
Grace Elizade-Utnick, *City University of New York at Brooklyn College*
Nancy Evangelista, *Alfred University*
Kathryn Fletcher, *Ball State University*
Randy Floyd, *University of Memphis*
Gilbert Foley, *New York Center for Child Development*
Laurie Ford, *University of British Columbia*
Pamela Guess, *University of Tennessee*
Robin Hojnoski, *Lehigh University*
Tammy Hughes (Associate Editor), *Duquesne University*
Paul McCabe, *Brooklyn College*
Sara McCane-Bowling, *University of Tennessee*
David McIntosh (Associate Editor), *Ball State University*
Barbara A. Mowder (Associate Editor), *Pace University*
Geraldine Oades-Sese, *Rutgers Robert Wood Johnson Medical School*
Matt Reynolds, *University of Kansas*
Gail Ross, *NY Presbyterian Hospital*
Flo Rubinson (Associate Editor), *Brooklyn College*
Susan Ruby, *Eastern Washington University*
Mark Sossin, *Pace University*
Esther Stavrou, *Yeshiva University*
Mark Terjesen, *St. John's University*
Lea Theodore, *College of William and Mary*
Mary Ward, *Weill Cornell Medical College*

Perspectives on Early Childhood Psychology and Education

Welcome to the newly named journal *Perspectives on Early Childhood Psychology and Education* (PECPE) published by Pace University Press. This journal replaces the *Journal of Early Childhood and Infant Psychology* (JECIP), which has not been published since 2012. All of us associated with PECPE are excited to launch the first issue in Spring 2016 with a special series on parenting along with two general articles. This first issue will be followed by a special series on Autism in Fall 2016, along with some general articles. This will be the format of PECPE; that is, two special issues a year edited by one of the journal's associate editors, that will also include a few general articles.

Editorial Policy and Submission Guidelines

Perspectives on Early Childhood Psychology and Education focuses on publishing original contributions from a broad range of psychological and educational perspectives relevant to infants, young children (to age 8 years), families, and caregivers. Manuscripts incorporating evidence-based research, theory, and practice within clinical, community, developmental, neurological, and school psychology perspectives are considered. In addition, the journal accepts test and book reviews, literature reviews, program descriptions and evaluations, clinical studies, and other professional materials of interest to psychologists and educators working with young children. Proposals for special focus topics may be made to the Editor.

Format: Manuscripts should be original work not currently submitted for publication to other journals. Authors must follow the guidelines of the Publication Manual of the American Psychological Association (Sixth Edition). Manuscripts may not exceed 35 double-spaced pages in length, including the cover page, abstract, references, tables and figures.

Submission: Submit an electronic copy of the manuscript for editorial review. Avoid including any identifying author information in the text. Selection of manuscripts is based on blind peer review. Include a cover page with the following information: the title of article, author(s) full name(s), title(s), institution or professional affiliations, and mailing and email address of primary author.

The cover page will not be sent to reviewers.

Selection Criteria:

- Importance of topic in early childhood psychology and education
- Theory and research related to content
- Contribution to professional practice in early childhood psychology and education
- Clear and concise writing

Submit manuscripts to the Editor at the following address:

Dr. Vincent C. Alfonso
Gonzaga University
School of Education
502 East Boone Avenue
Spokane, WA 99258

Email: PECPE@gonzaga.edu

TABLE OF CONTENTS

Welcome to *Perspectives* ix
Vincent C. Alfonso

SPECIAL FOCUS:
PARENTING AND YOUNG CHILDREN

Introduction to Parenting Issue 1
Barbara A. Mowder and Renee Krochek

Parenting History, Contemporary Views,
and the Parent Development Theory:
Implications for Early Childhood Providers 5
Barbara A. Mowder

The Parent Development Theory:
Empirical Support 27
Renee Krochek and Barbara A. Mowder

Contemporary Parenting:
The Influence of Screen Time on Parenting and Children 39
Alixandra Blackman and Linda Olszewski

Structuring and Supporting Healthy Child Development:
Parenting Practices in Relation to Feeding and Screen Time ..79
Jessica Retan and Allison M. Hill

Screen Time Questionnaire:
Measuring Parents' and Children's Media Use 109
Linda Olszewski, Shagufta Asar, Ashley Bogatch, and
Alixandra Blackman

LIST OF CONTRIBUTORS 137

GENERAL ARTICLES

Evaluation of a Modified Check-in/Check-out Intervention
for Young Children 143
*Zachary LaBrot, Brad Dufrene, Keith Radley,
and Jamie Pasqua*

Field-validation of the COMET Mentoring Model to Enhance
the Instructional Practices of Head Start Teachers 167
*Stephen J. Bagnato, Jai Wha Seo, Jennifer Salaway, and
Myoung Soon Kim*

Welcome to Perspectives

Welcome to *Perspectives on Early Childhood Psychology and Education* (PECPE)! This is the first issue of the newly named journal published by Pace University Press. As many of you know the former name of the journal was the *Journal of Early Child and Infant Psychology* (JECIP). The associate editors, namely, Tammy Hughes, David McIntosh, Barbara Mowder, and Florence Rubinson, and I are delighted to launch the new journal after several years of dormancy and preparation. We are joined by more than 30 editorial review board members, myself, and Manuela Soares who assumed the position of Associate Director of Pace University Press. Manuela has been instrumental in assisting all of us to resume publishing in the fields of early childhood psychology and education.

The scope of *Perspectives* remains similar to that of JECIP. Specifically, the new journal focuses on publishing original contributions from a broad range of psychological and educational perspectives relevant to infants, young children (to age 8 years), families, and caregivers. Manuscripts incorporating evidence-based research, theory, and practice within clinical, community, developmental, neurological, and school psychology perspectives are considered. In addition, the journal accepts test and book reviews, literature reviews, program descriptions and evaluations, clinical studies, and other professional materials of interest to psychologists and educators working with young children. Proposals for special focus topics may be made to the Editor. *Perspectives* will be published two times per year (typically spring and fall/winter). Each issue will have a special focus and general articles. In this first issue, the special focus is on parenting and young children and was edited by Barbara Mowder and Renee Krochek. The articles in this special series address parent development theory, development of the screen time questionnaire, the influence of screen time on parents and children, and parenting practices in relation to feeding and screen time. The two general articles in this inaugural issue of

Perspectives address the relative effectiveness of check-in/check-out in early childhood settings and a structured, individualized, and relationship-based teacher mentoring model named COMET.

In the next issue of *Perspectives* (Fall 2016), the special focus will be on autism and mental health. That volume will be edited by David McIntosh.

In closing I hope you find *Perspectives* to be a useful journal in your research and practice. Please feel free to contact me with ideas, comments, and suggestions. We are very open to innovative ideas and look forward to hearing from you.

Enjoy *Perspectives*!

— Vincent C. Alfonso, Ph.D.
Editor

SPECIAL FOCUS
==

Parenting and Young Children

Introduction to Parenting and Young Children

Barbara A. Mowder and Renee Krochek

We are very pleased to offer this focus on parenting and young children for the inaugural issue of *Perspectives in Early Childhood Psychology and Education*. This issue represents the accumulated work of many individuals who are or have been a part of the Parent Child Institute (PCI) at Pace University in New York City. The PCI was founded in 2012, primarily as an academic research institute located at Pace University in lower Manhattan. Since the beginning, the goals of the PCI have been to foster research on parents and children and to disseminate research findings. This issue represents contributions toward those initial PCI goals.

Each of these articles represents substantial thought regarding parenting, and many of the ideas in the articles have been presented as individual papers, posters, and/or symposiums at professional organizations such as the American Psychological Association and the National Association of School Psychologists. This issue begins with the article entitled "Parenting History, Contemporary Views, and the Parent Development Theory: Implications for Early Childhood Providers." This article provides an overview of parenting thought from ancient times to the present, focusing on the varying perspectives regarding the parent role. The article provides historical examples of parenting in conjunction with use of the more contemporary parent development theory (PDT). The PDT is a recent theory of parenting that provides a framework for practitioners to conceptualize how they and the parents they work with consider the parent role. This article forms the context in which the following articles expand thinking about parents.

In the next article, "The Parent Development Theory: Empirical Support," Krochek and Mowder talk further about the PDT and present the empirical basis for the seven parent role characteristics (e.g., bonding, discipline), explore the development of parenting beliefs across the lifespan, and present the correlation between parenting practices and beliefs. Regarding the basis for the seven parent role characteristics, statistical analyses support the PDT parent role structure. In terms of parenting beliefs across the lifespan, research studies affirm the assertion that there are differences in importance ratings for parent role characteristics across children's developmental levels. Finally, the measures of parenting associated with the PDT (e.g., frequency of parent behaviors, importance of parent behaviors) are strongly correlated with each other, indicating a relationship between parenting beliefs and parenting behavior.

In the next article, "Contemporary Parenting: The Influence of Screen Time on Parenting and Children," Blackman and Olszewski closely examine the influence of screen time on parents and children. In general, the article provides a history of technology and child development outcomes along with a presentation of the increasingly expansive role technology plays within parents' and children's lives. There is a historical account of technology in the 20th century as well as an analysis of contemporary screen-time research. Blackman and Olszewski delineate the impact of technology on play, one of the most important ways that children develop cognitive and social skills. Thoughtfully addressing issues such as the quantity and quality of screen time, the authors offer some recommendations for parents and those working with parents.

Subsequently, the following article, "Structuring and Supporting Healthy Child Development: Parenting Practices in Relation to Feeding and Screen Time," addresses issues related to parenting and children's nutrition. In this article, Retan and Hill tackle an important parenting issue of contemporary concern, particularly because of the high number of children in the United States who are overweight or obese. The authors provide a sense of some of the issues, such as the marketing of high-calorie low-nutrition drinks and food items to children, that abound. In addition, they weigh feeding and nutrition in conjunction with screen time, offering a rich perspective on the many facets of childhood weight and health issues.

In the final article, "Screen Time Questionnaire: Measuring Parents' and Children's Media Use," Olszewski, Asar, Bogatch, and Blackman consider the wide range of technology that is increasingly available to parents and their children. These authors go on to describe the development of a psychometrically sound measure, the Screen Time Questionnaire (STQ), to assess the use of technology by parents and children, individually and in terms of the parent-child dyadic relationship. The measure provides a tool for psychologists and others to discern the potential risks associated with overuse of technology.

Taken as a whole, the articles on parenting and young children offer early childhood professionals a synopsis of some of the important issues practitioners face in meeting the needs of young children and their families. From the historical conceptualization of what it means to be a parent through one contemporary theory on parenting, practitioners are provided with a theoretical basis for their ideas of parenting. Next, contemporary issues are explored that relate to the use of technology in terms of parent-child relationships and child development outcomes, while measuring that usage, as well as to nutritional issues (and screen time) and ways to foster positive child growth and development.

This special focus is meant to provide a broad, as well as specific, view of parenting while exploring issues historically and currently at play. Within the realm of clinical practice, mental health and other early childhood professionals often are called upon to be knowledgeable in a wide array of areas. Because practitioners who are focused on the needs of children often work with their parents and families as well, a solid grasp of the parenting literature is important. Understanding the literature historically, for example, the seminal work of Diana Baumrind, as well as contemporarily (e.g., the PDT) equips practitioners to work competently with parents while understanding the intricacies at play. Being knowledgeable about cutting edge issues, such as screen time and nutrition, is similarly important. Mental health and other early childhood professionals are looked to for guidance and information about child development outcomes. Understanding current technologies, for example, and how their use impacts children of various ages will allow practitioners to work more effectively with the clients and families that they serve. As a whole, this special focus is meant to sensitize practitioners to some of the many issues inherent in providing services to young children and their families.

Parenting History, Contemporary Views, and the Parent Development Theory: Implications for Early Childhood Providers

Barbara A. Mowder

Abstract

To facilitate an appreciation of parents, parenting, and the parent role, the author begins by presenting a historical synopsis of parenting beliefs from ancient times to the present. Understanding that parent-role perceptions are not universal, but rather housed in place, time, and personal circumstances, can facilitate practitioners' awareness of the perspectives of parents with whom they work. Using the cognitive-behavioral based Parent Development Theory (PDT), this article makes the case that parents and early childhood practitioners interact with each other within the context of their social roles. The PDT provides early childhood practitioners with a path for conceptualizing and working with parents in meaningful ways. The implications of utilizing the PDT for practice and theory are drawn.

Key words: parent role, parenting, parent history, parent development theory, parent education

Since parents not only are the responsible agents for their young children, but also act as the conduit between those needing services and the professionals who provide them, addressing their parenting role is relevant. Take, for example, the Asian American mother whose cultural background prizes and idealizes the female who keeps the family home spotless and attends to her husband's every need yet whose young child has learning difficulties and attention deficit hyperactivity disorder (ADHD) that need to be attended to. Or, the overwhelmed father who is struggling with grief regarding the recent loss of an infant yet who has three other children who need his attention. Finally, the mother who props up an infant in the corner of the couch and positions the bottle in the baby's arms so the infant can feed and learn to be independent at the same time. How does the practitioner work with the mother who prizes housekeeping over meeting the needs of her child, the grieving father who has other young children who need him, or the mother determined to teach her youngster independence while providing nutrition? In each instance, the practitioner needs to appreciate what the individual parent values within a culturally sensitive context, weigh those perceptions in light of the needs of young children and their families, and communicate effectively within the parent-practitioner dynamic. In the end, the parenting discussion presented here serves as a mechanism for mental health professionals and other early childhood practitioners to conceptualize and think about parents' roles, as well as their own, in constructing a meaningful path for providing services to young children and their families.

Getting a sense of parenting beliefs, as they have emerged over time, provides a backdrop for understanding contemporary parent role complexities. In this article, the historical picture is broadly drawn, acknowledging the inherent difficulties of capturing all possible parenting perspectives, by moving from a dependence on diverse writers and related historical sources to the parenting ideas and perspectives co-emergent with psychology as a science in the 20th and 21st centuries. The goal of this article is not to provide a comprehensive examination of the construct of parenting, but rather to offer the reader some understanding, appreciation, and overviews of parenting as previously conceptualized; at the same time, the aim is to bring forth recent perspectives, including the cognitive, behaviorally framed parent development theory (PDT), to draw implications for professional practice.

Historical Overview

Presenting even a selective overview of parenting beliefs and behaviors over time is a daunting task. Historical records specifically focused on parenting are rare and not easy to locate, and, even when available, they are subject to a contemporary lens focused on ideas and actions that surely were housed and had their own meaning in time and place. Overriding many of the problems faced when trying to understand and capture that which is not within our immediate grasp is the vexing issue that the parenting records that do exist were produced mostly by men and not by the women who were performing the parent role and associated tasks. Although concern regarding who wrote what is generally relevant with regard to any aspect of history, the history of parenting begs a number of issues. Valerie French (1995), for example, succinctly makes this point by noting that parenting-related behaviors and tasks generally fell to women, but their voices are not historically recorded. In other words, whatever was thought or recorded about parenting was written about or depicted primarily by men and, therefore, does not necessarily represent the women who were more directly involved.

Much of the history of the parenting portion of this article, ancient times through the 17th century, utilizes secondary sources (e.g., Airèes, 1962; French, 1995), since a detailed historical consideration of parenting is beyond the scope of this article. Subsequently, from the 18th century through late 19th century, and then again in the 20th and 21st centuries, primary sources of writing and research are relied upon most. Altogether, the historical discussion is intended to provide a background within which early childhood practitioners can think about the myriad ways parenting has been conceptualized over time. The historical references can sensitize early childhood providers to the range of parenting perspectives and conceivable distortions based on issues such as individuals' own experiences in parent-child relationships and their social-cultural upbringing.

When practitioners sit down with parents in front of them, they are talking with individuals who have their own perceptions of what is important in terms of parenting and whose ideas have been framed by various conscious and unconscious influences.

Ancient Times

French (1995) exquisitely points to the lack of women's voices, and a multitude of other issues, in her work on the history of parenting in the ancient Mediterranean and Near Eastern worlds. The history French presents, by offering extensive, thoughtful, and historically meaningful comments about child care and parenting, lends weight to how parenting is conceptualized in this article. French specifically notes that although she is writing on parenting there are actually four lines of inquiry, not mutually exclusive, regarding the family: child rearing, family, history of childhood, and parenting. In her pursuit of the history of parenting, she also observes how difficult it is to sort through parenting definitions and related materials. For instance, French offers the example of the ancient Greek play by Aeschylus in which Apollo declares, "The mother is no parent of that which is called/her child, but only the nurse of the new-planted seed/that grows. The parent is he who mounts. A stranger, she preserves a stranger's seed" (*Eumenides*, as cited in French, 1995, p. 264). This view of the mother, as parent, serves as a convenient vehicle within the play to assuage the guilt of Orestes, who kills his mother, is tormented by the furies, and suffers the judgment of others. Even though this historical artifact of the parent role is distinctive and certainly works within the play, to generalize the definition to one universally held by Athenians would be beyond problematic. However, this serves as an example of one of various points of view regarding parents and parenting from a distant time.

With historical caveats in mind, French narrows her discussion to parenting in the ancient Near East and Mediterranean worlds and quickly acknowledges that parenting was not a unified construct since parental expectations varied not only between individuals, but also across socioeconomic class and subcultures. For example, evidence from ancient Egypt, including literary works and artistic depictions, generally presents children as integral members of families and parents as affectionate and caring toward their children. In contrast, in ancient Mesopotamia literary or artistic presentations of parents with children seem almost nonexistent, leading some to wonder if child rearing and parenting carried some negative connotations and/or were viewed as burdensome. French notes that making assertions about parenting in ancient Mesopotamia may not make sense since few scholars familiar with this ancient culture have focused specifically on the topics of child rearing, family, or parenting.

The ancient Greeks, at least those with access to the thinking of the times, clearly were conversant with child developmental issues (French, 1995). The literary legacy from both Plato and Aristotle is replete with references to stages of child development and the importance of responding to children's changing developmental needs. For instance, Plato placed special emphasis on parenting during infancy, characterizing infants' perceptions of pleasure and pain as stepping-stones to developing a sense of right and wrong and to overall moral development. There were other well-formulated ideas of children as well as of the differences between children and adults in terms of the body and the mind. Parental responses to children's changing needs were expected in the community and general society.

Finally, the Romans, with their emphasis on *familia* (i.e., the bringing together of children, fathers, mothers, associated kin, chattel, and so forth), apparently parented somewhat similarly to the Greeks with, perhaps, the possible exception that the father had an apparently fearsome degree or level of control over his family, including the right to kill his own children. French (1995) notes that historians think at some point between the start of the second century and the close of the first century BCE, Romans' views of young children underwent a significant shift. The change seems to represent an increased emphasis on the affective bonds between parents and their children, perhaps part of recognizing and/or acknowledging parental mourning over the death of young children.

To be sure, the ancient Mediterranean world is important for being the seat of extensive philosophical writing and learning, yet it is but one place in the world where parenting was thought about and taking place. There were parenting beliefs and practices from known and unknown lands other than Western cultures, which are not part of the overview of parenting in this article, many of which may or may not be recorded in historically accessible ways and some, therefore, are lost to time. Before French, Ariès attempted a comprehensive consideration of family life over time. Drawing on historical artifacts (e.g., drawings, paintings) and findings (e.g., documents from the past), Ariès (1962) notes that he pieced together "references to things which were too ordinary, too commonplace, too far removed from the memorable incident for contemporary writers to mention" (p. 10).

For example, Ariès made the assertion that in medieval times young children were coddled, and then, at a certain point in their development, they were considered small adults. Pointing to evidence from the 10th century, he maintains that artists had a hard time presenting children as anything other than small women or men. He goes on to consider such things as art and family portraits, medieval texts, and narratives in poetry in constructing an elaborate impression of what parenting and families were like. He goes on to wonder how "ignorance of childhood" changed into the 19th century view of the child as the center of family life. Ariès systematically proposes an evolution of the conceptualization of children and family life, and his contributions in this regard have been widely appreciated. Indeed, his work is often credited as one of the first attempts at trying to conceptualize centuries of children, family lives, and parents. At the same time, some of his assertions, particularly those about the notion of childhood not having been thought about or appreciated until the 19th century, have been soundly criticized.

In appreciating a sense of parenting over time, French (1995), Ariès (1962), and so many others (e.g., Thompson, Hogan, & Clark, 2012), recognize the obstacles (e.g., limited records, limited sources) imposed on history. In consideration of those concerns, the further discussion of parenting picks up in the 18th century with Jean-Jacques Rousseau (1712-1778), who presented a distinctive point of view on child development and rearing.

Pre- to Co-Scientific Times

Rousseau was not the first, most persuasive, or most comprehensive author regarding parents and children, but he does provide a convenient point of departure to discuss parents and parenting. His oft-cited text, *Émile* (1762), might be cast as an early attempt to delineate the scope and range of the conditions for child rearing. One of the reasons Rousseau is so important is that he comes to the many issues of educating children from such a specific perspective. In *Émile*, Rousseau draws an elaborate portrait of the idealized child, Émile, and Émile's perfect, hypothetical education and, by extension, upbringing. In the treatise, Rousseau elaborates upon every detail of care and attention toward Émile's upbringing, only introducing formal education as the child himself indicates an interest and readiness. He lavishes attention on Émile's growth, giving evidence of a keen eye and sense of perception regarding Émile's extensive developmental twists and turns. Always encouraging the reader to join him in wonder and intense interest in Émile's flowering development, Rousseau outlines exactly what constitutes optimum rearing or training.

This lofty discourse, parenthetically, stands in stark contradistinction to Rousseau's treatment of his own children. By all accounts, and verified in Rousseau's *Confessions* (1782), he demanded that Thérèse his apparently illiterate housekeeper and toward the end of his life his wife, give up each of their five babies. The first such disposal (his words, or that of the translator as recorded in his *Confessions*) was made over Thérèse's tearful objections. This infant was sent to the Paris Foundling Hospital, an almost certain death sentence, with an embroidered "R" on a piece of material tucked inside his swaddling clothes. The other four babies did not enjoy the same level of consideration. Later in life, Rousseau's friends encouraged exploration about what happened to the children, but apparently no information could be ascertained at that point. In the *Confessions* tome, references to his children occur in only about three paragraphs scattered throughout the book. In the end, perhaps Rousseau's propositions reflect either his own upbringing, with related regrets, or simply aspirational thoughts regarding education rather than necessarily suggesting actual upbringing.

Skipping forward to the 19th century, there were various child-rearing pamphlets produced, some from religious leaders and others by physicians, many of which focused on children's moral development. At the end of 19th century, Emmett Holt (1855-1924), a pediatrician, wrote on the care and feeding of children (1894); originally put together as a training manual for nurses, his work became the most published child-care manual during the early part of the 20th century (Thompson et al., 2012). Much of his material was specifically related to general child developmental expectations, but other portions do seem odd to modern eyes, such as suggesting toilet training by age three months, discouraging rocking a baby, and cautioning against playing with children before they are six months of age. Coincident with Holt's work, interest in parents and parenting surged during the early part of the 20th century, particularly due to concerns over the high rate of infant mortality.

Twentieth Century

Restricting the time frame considerably, Lomax, Kagan, and Rosenkrantz (1978) took a focused view on parenting by looking at the science and patterns of child care from the 19th century through much of the 20th century. They capture some of the strikingly diverse points of view promulgated regarding parenting and the ideal family life. Writing in the 1970s, these authors maintain that thinking about parenting had shifted dramatically in the past century:

> Only 60 years ago many American mothers believed that infants were fragile creatures who should not be handled frequently or overstimulated lest the stress of that intrusion damage their internal balance. Only 25 years ago millions of American mothers believed that anxiety, anger, shame, or guilt about nursing, weaning, toilet training, and masturbation could prevent a child from realizing his intellectual and emotional potential. I recall hearing of a parent who told the college girl who was sitting with her infant to make sure that the infant did not see his feces when she changed his diapers because the trauma of viewing his squashed bodily product might scar him. (p. IX-X)

Tracking the first empirical studies of child rearing and the psychosocial development of infants, these writers detail the early contributions of G. Stanley Hall (1844-1924), who attempted to accumulate masses of data, but ultimately failed to answer larger developmental questions. They go on to recognize many others, especially enumerating the many influences that Sigmund Freud had on conceptualizations of parenting. For example, Freud questioned the strong calls for strict infant early training and directed attention toward facets of children's personality development, which had been mostly overlooked.

Stepping back a bit, early in the 20th century in the United States, President Theodore Roosevelt embraced and championed the idea of a Children's Bureau and forwarded this proposal to Congress in 1909. Along with two national conferences regarding children and parents, these efforts did result in the creation of the Children's Bureau, signed into law in 1912 by President William Howard Taft (Pickren, Dewsbury, & Wertheimer, 2012; Thompson et al., 2012). The Bureau's early efforts focused on infant mortality, and the first publication was on prenatal care, followed closely by manuals on infant care.

Coincident to attention focused on children at the federal level was the increasing development of psychology as a science of prediction and control and, more specifically, the beginnings of institutionalization of developmental psychology as a field within academic psychology (Pickren et al., 2012). Specific child study began at settings such as the Iowa Child Welfare Station at the University of Iowa (1917), the Merrill-Palmer School in Detroit (1920), and Teachers College at Columbia University in New York City. Philanthropy supported much of the early research in child development and parent education, with striking contributions from the Laura Spelman Rockefeller Memorial (LSRM). Beginning in 1923, Lawrence K. Frank was tasked with allocating one million dollars annually to further knowledge about children. Pickren et al. (2012) note that funds were used to support the already established Iowa Child Welfare Research Station and also were distributed to Teachers College at Columbia University, the University of California at Berkeley, the University of Minnesota, and the University of Toronto to establish new institutes. One of many results of this funding was the development of *The Parent's Magazine* as an informational outlet and a vehicle for educating parents.

One of the most important and influential early contributors to parenting and child rearing at this time was Arnold Gesell (1880-1961), arguably the foremost expert from the 1920s to the 1950s (Weizmann & Harris, 2012). Well trained in psychology as well as pediatrics, Gesell carefully collected data on children from different developmental levels, filming much of his work and writing solid developmentally based books, such as *Infancy and Human Growth* (1928). Although Gesell took a decidedly biological, maturational perspective regarding child development, when it came to parenting and children's personalities, he generally wove together behavioral concepts with some of the wisdom of William James and others (Weizmann & Harris, 2012). Beyond research and writing, Gesell is credited with blending psychology and education in practice, being the first individual with the title of school psychologist in the United States. In the end, where parenting and child development were concerned, Gesell tipped the scales on the side of nature while at the same time making ample allowance for environmental influences.

At about the same time as Gesell, but sprinting far in advance of the emerging literature on child development and parenting, John Broadus Watson (1878-1961) wrote *Psychological Care of Infant and Child* in 1928. Exhibiting reverence for the work of Ivan Pavlov and generalizing significantly from his own training and background in animal research, he maintained a strict behavioral perspective related to child rearing. Watson, writing especially in the 1920s and 1930s, had a striking impact on parenting thought (Thompson et al., 2012). Having had a poor upbringing in South Carolina, economically as well as in terms of family dysfunction, Watson struggled academically and socially, but he ultimately entered the University of Chicago for graduate education. Studying with some of the finest minds of the time, he became passionate about Pavlov and the implications associated with behaviorism. Although his training was mostly in experimental psychology and his dissertation on the training of rats, he was not deterred from applying his zeal for behaviorism wholesale to child development. He eschewed affectional bonds, favoring instead a matter-of-fact attitude toward children, even sarcastically dedicating his *Psychological Care of Infant and Child* (1928) "To the first mother who brings up a happy child." Watson (1930) is renowned for his famous statement regarding parenting:

Give me a dozen healthy infants, well-formed, and my own specified world to bring them up in and I'll guarantee to take any one at random and train him to become any type of specialist I might select – doctor, lawyer, artist, merchant-chief and, yes, even beggar-man and thief, regardless of his talents, penchants, tendencies, abilities, vocations, and race of his ancestors. I am going beyond my facts and I admit it, but so have the advocates of the contrary and they have been doing it for many thousands of years. (p. 82)

His book the *Psychological Care of Infant and Child* (Watson, 1928), written with the assistance of Rosalie Rayner, immediately sold well; apparently, more than 100,000 copies were sold over the first few months. Invigorated by the success of his ideas and, perhaps, a romantic involvement with his graduate assistant, Rayner, Watson had plans to advance his child rearing ideas. One key idea apparently involved an engineered nursery at Johns Hopkins Hospital with room for 40 infants, which seemingly received significant, enthusiastic support from his colleagues. According to most accounts, when his affair with his graduate assistant became widely known, any academic aspirations Watson had had were quickly terminated. He was summarily fired from Johns Hopkins, but quickly morphed his profession in academics into an advertising career on Madison Avenue in New York City. Raynor became his wife, they had two children, and in 1930 she wistfully wrote in *The Parent's Magazine* about the realities and compromises of raising children in a structured behavioral household in which play and displays of affection were discouraged. For example, parties and special occasions were rare and any physical displays of affection, such as hugging, frowned upon and strongly discouraged (Watson, 1930). J. B. Watson, in sharp contrast to Gesell, held a decidedly nurture perspective in terms of child rearing.

Some two decades later, Benjamin Spock (1903-1998), a pediatrician with psychoanalytic training, became an unbelievably successful parenting expert with the publication of *The Common Sense Book of Baby and Child Care* in 1946. Spock depended on stage models of development and, according to Weizmann and Harris (2012), was influenced by Gesell and Ilg's (1943) *Infant and Child in the Culture of Today*. Spock's general style as a professional parenting-advice provider came across as warm, supportive, and understanding. His emphasis was on being flexible in parenting; this was not an insight on Spock's part since this idea, too, had come from Gesell, the first advocate of flexible parenting. Bringing together medical knowledge, in conjunction with psychoanalytic training and other child developmental expertise, Spock was well received and by most accounts wildly popular, as evidenced by his books being translated widely and outsold only by the Bible for much of the 20th century.

Not far from Spock in terms of psychodynamic underpinnings, John Bowlby (1907-1990) and Mary Ainsworth (1913-1999), moved the parenting and child rearing conversation forward with their research and publications considering infant attachment in conjunction with maternal deprivation. Writing extensively on the importance of mothers or a mother-substitute in an infant's life, Bowlby published *Maternal Care and Mental Health* in 1951. Ainsworth and Bowlby subsequently collaborated and produced *Child Care and the Birth of Love* in 1965, and Ainsworth later formulated a classification system for attachment styles. The net effect of their work was the emphasis on the mother, or mother-substitute, someone consistently responsive to the child. Although their work focused on the child end of the parent-child dyadic relationship, in terms of classifying secure, insecure, or disorganized child attachment, the implications for parenting were very clear. The infant needs at least one adult who is attuned to the infant's many behaviors that are calculated to keep the parent near. The implication was that infants and young children require someone close by at all times, someone sensitive and responsive to their needs, and the implication was that that someone was the mother.

Up to this point in time, most philosophical writings, pediatric as well as other advice pamphlets/manuals, and the psychological sciences consistently pointed to the mother as the key figure in terms of parenting. The mother was not only conceptualized as the provider of parenting, but, in addition, the causative factor if anything went wrong (Eyer, 1992). In this vein entered Drs. John Kennell (1922-2013) and Marshall Klaus (born 1927), two pediatricians who, with other researchers, made a sensation in 1970 and 1972 with their research studies published in *The New England Journal of Medicine* and *Pediatrics*. Looking at parenting primarily from a biological and instinctual point of view, in what might be characterized as a reductionistic manner, they honed in on maternal behavior from the first contact of a mother with "her young" to the importance of the first postpartum days. Drawing on nonhuman research and amplifying their ideas based on poorly designed studies, Kennell and Klaus caused a sensation with their book, addressed both to professionals and parents, entitled *Maternal-infant Bonding: The Impact of Early Separation or Loss on Family Development* (1976). They strongly embraced a number of unsupported assertions regarding the attachment process, including, for instance, that some crucial elements of attachment were said to include a "sensitive period" shortly after birth in which babies needed close physical contact with their mother. Eyer (1992) severely objected to their premises:

> By selecting the behavior of a few species of animals that coincided with popular notions about women's maternal "instinct," bonding research reduced women to automatons who behave the way they do, not because of their capacity to reason, their complex psychology, or their economic or social circumstances, but rather because of their inherent and inevitable inferiority. This inferiority then requires the full services of science and medicine to guide it. (p. 5-6)

There were positive and negative outcomes associated with the positions of Kennell and Klaus. On the positive side, hospitals across the country changed their birthing procedures, and parents were allowed and actually encouraged to hold their infants soon after birth. The effect on birth protocols is most frequently mentioned as the outstanding contribution of Kennell and Klaus. On the negative side, there were the outcries and suffering endured by adoptive and other parents whose children had not enjoyed direct physical touch after birth (e.g., those whose infants had received NICU services), who had presumably missed the "sensitive period" and therefore, to some, were damaged or doomed for life (Eyer, 1992).

Kennell and Klaus, building on Bowlbyism (e.g., keeping mothers of children in the home) as well as Harry Harlow's compelling research in the 1950s on the detrimental effects of maternal deprivation on infant rhesus monkeys, constructed a seemingly invincible case for mothers having direct responsibility for raising their children. Indeed, their bonding research, deeply housed within attachment theory, paved the way for maintaining that mothers should stay in the home due to the need for physical proximity between mother and child. Striking back, many women were skeptical of the implication that they should be the ones to remain at home with their children, be unpaid for their labor, and forego the financial, intellectual, social, and other rewards associated with the workplace. Smarting from the unsubstantiated assertions and upset by the public outcry, including loud complaints from the psychological research community, Kennell and Klaus substantially modified many of their claims (Kennell & Klaus, 1984; Klaus & Kennell, 1983).

Somewhat parallel to the evolving perspectives of Spock, Bowlby and Ainsworth, and even Kennell and Klaus, many psychologists began conducting research pointing out differential aspects of parenting. One example would be the work of Diana Baumrind (e.g., 1966, 1967, 1971), who carefully studied and outlined different parenting styles based on two continuums: demandingness/control and responsiveness/warmth. The two continuums eventually led

Baumrind and others to assert and articulate four parenting styles: authoritarian (high demandingness/control, low responsiveness/warmth), authoritative (high demandingness/control, high responsiveness/warmth), permissive (low demandingness/control, high responsiveness/warmth), and neglectful (low demandingness/control, low responsiveness/warmth). Continued research in this vein conducted by Baumrind, as well as many others, lent support to the authoritative style in terms of optimum child developmental outcomes (e.g., content with self, explorative, self-controlled, self-reliant) and points out child developmental difficulties associated with the authoritarian style (e.g., discontented, distrustful, withdrawn) and the permissive style (e.g., least explorative, self-controlled, or self-reliant).

Contemporary Views

During the last part of the 20th century and into the 21st century, there were and are few specific theories addressing the issue of parents and related parenting behaviors. Ellen Galinsky (1987) developed her "Six Stages of Parenthood" from an early childhood education perspective and suggested that parents go through stages of parenting, from imagining the child prior to the infant's birth through the departure stage when the child leaves the home to start his or her own family. This theory has limited use in professional practice and research. Instead, toward the end of the century, there are scant additional parenting theories for researchers and practitioners to rely on.

Relatively recently, the author of this article developed and has written about the parent development theory (PDT) in order to define and conceptualize who parents are, incorporate what they do, and consider how, what, when, and where behaviors that are associated with parenting occur (Mowder, 2005). In essence, the parent is defined as the individual who recognizes, accepts, and performs the parent role. The parent role, based on research (e.g., Mowder, Harvey, Pedro, Rossen, & Moy, 1993; Mowder, Harvey,

Moy, & Pedro, 1995) and modified somewhat over time, includes behaviors associated with bonding (e.g., warmth and caring), discipline (e.g., establishing and following through with expectations and rules), education (e.g., informing and teaching children), general welfare and protection (e.g., providing necessities and assuring safety), responsivity (e.g., responding to children), and sensitivity (e.g., attunement of responses to children's needs), along with negativity (e.g., demeaning or hurting children).

The PDT considers parenting in conjunction with individuals' development of their cognitive perspectives on parenting. That is, typically from the time individuals are young children, they recognize that there are different social roles (e.g., family roles, gender roles) and form ideas of what those roles entail. In this vein, parent role conceptualizations begin early and are modified over time according to individual parents' characteristics (e.g., age, education, prior experiences in a parent-child relationship) as well as children's characteristics (e.g., age, special needs), the parent-child interaction, family dynamics, and the social-cultural context. Along with cognitive development and the increased nuances of parent role perspectives, individuals also form thoughts regarding behaviors associated with importance levels of certain parent-role characteristics (e.g., the relative importance of discipline for elementary-aged children in contrast to infants). In general, therefore, there is correspondence to some degree between what parents think and what they do about parenting. The PDT is a stage-based theory, and the supposition is that parent role characteristics (e.g., bonding, discipline, education) vary in importance according to children's developmental levels (e.g., infant/toddler, preschool, elementary school aged, adolescents) in general, and, more specifically, according to individual children's needs, the parent-child dyadic relationship, family dynamics, and the values and/or imperatives extant within the social-cultural milieu.

The PDT, although for the most part original in terms of conceptualizing parenting by specifying definitions and utilizing a cognitive developmental and social learning framework, is far from novel. Some of the earliest philosophers, such as Plato, were considering issues related to child rearing in accordance with children's developmental needs. The PDT not only is consistent with aspects of child-rearing thought over time, but also fits into the stream of parenting research and theory by incorporating, for example, parent social role characteristics in conjunction with children's nature and nurture. Furthermore, the PDT recognizes and incorporates dynamic changes that occur in parenting thought and behavior over time, as in general systems theory (e.g., von Bertalanffy), within a Bronfenbrenner (1979) (e.g., microsystem, mesosystem, exosystem, macrosystem) type of overall framework.

Implications for Early Childhood Providers

From a historical perspective, then, the parent role has been conceptualized in a myriad of ways. For example, from ancient times through contemporary perspectives, the role has been cast as a mostly biologically driven phenomenon (e.g., Aeschylus, Gesell, Kennell and Klaus) or a role under environmental control (e.g., Watson) or some combination of approaches (e.g., Bowlby, Spock). Some cultures seem to have emphasized the importance of affection (e.g., ancient Egypt), while bonds of affection are more difficult to discern in others (e.g., ancient Mesopotamia). Looking at contemporary views, there have been significant changes in thinking with regard to issues such as maternal and paternal contributions to parenting (e.g., from concerns over maternal deprivation and instinctual maternal drives to a more balanced perspective), adherence to schedules, and the importance of flexibility.

Appreciating the historical multitude of perspectives, sometimes discrepant, at times nuanced, some recently supported by research and some not, provides a glimpse of some of the issues at play when considering parents and parenting. Notable in this article is the reliance on Western culture, economic, and social influences that color the historical and current picture of parenting. Taking that into account, and incorporating the early 20th century's use of psychology as a science to establish the relationship between parenting and child development outcomes (e.g., the Laura Spelman Rockefeller Memorial), there still is no agreed upon, more or less, parenting template. Instead, in general, parenting is individually conceptualized by those performing the parent role as well as by professionals who work with parents. As a result, the possibilities abound for professionals to assume they "know" the parent role, to apply their preconceptions to those with whom they work, and to potentially misunderstand those individual parents with whom they work. Ultimately, each individual who performs the parent role or works with parents does so based on a myriad of factors, such as his or her own upbringing, education, experiences in parent-child dyadic and family relationships, and socio-cultural background.

Revisiting the mother who embraces homemaking and cleanliness over meeting the important needs of her child, the grieving father who struggles to attend to his other children's needs, and the mother who is working on her infant's preparation for independence, the practitioner might begin a hypothetical professional relationship by getting a sense of the individual parent's priorities and assessing the correspondence with parent role importance (e.g., bonding, discipline, education) in conjunction with the child's needs and development level. The PDT, for example, provides a framework for such professional practice work with parents. The first step in that process would be appraising the individual's perception of their parent role; in this regard, there are parenting measures associated with the PDT (Mowder & Shamah, 2012).

Recognizing the differences of opinion and shifts in parenting perspectives may give professionals pause in their work with parents and families. That is, the historical issues are as alive today as ever, especially for early childhood practitioners who increasingly work with diverse family constellations, cultural differences, and some, perhaps, deeply ingrained parenting thoughts. The pause and thoughtful consideration, in turn, provides professionals with the time and consideration necessary to be sensitive regarding how individual parents are thinking about themselves and their children. Because of changes in the parent role, lack of current parenting consensus, and potential discrepant perceptions between parents and professionals regarding the parent role, there may be wide opportunities for miscommunication and misunderstanding between professionals and parents that the thoughtful practitioner can avoid.

At this juncture, weighing what individual parents' priorities are and how their parenting conceptualizations and behaviors match their goals may be sensitive as well as useful in effectively meeting children's needs. To the extent that professionals can understand and speak to parents' goals, psychological and other services may be enhanced and the needs of young children, their parents, and families met. In terms of assessment, for example, a focus strictly on children (e.g., using the BASC-2, WISC-V) might fail to take into account the importance of the parenting children are receiving. What if children are experiencing social-emotional difficulties and their parent is providing little attention or guidance? In terms of consultation, what if the service provider is recommending a course of action (e.g., spending more time reading to the child) in terms that conflict with other aspects of their role (e.g., taking time away from other children, family interactions, other activities)? What about the parent with deeply held, developmentally questionable beliefs regarding desirable child outcomes? In each of these, and ultimately all cases of psychological services, the skilled early childhood professional is wise to consider the parents' as well as their own parenting views regarding nuances associated with the role.

Issues with regard to the parent role have ramifications in terms of professional services, which, in turn, depend on psychological research and theory. Therefore, there are implications for research (e.g., what parenting characteristics are associated with positive child development outcomes at what points in children's development) as well as practice (e.g., how to sequence work with parents to sensitively provide services to young children). Research and theory are necessary to provide a contextual framework for thinking about individuals and the important social role of parents. With such a backdrop, providers can think about many issues that potentially influence parents (e.g., nutrition, screen time) and work with parents to optimize parenting behaviors and positive child development outcomes.

References

Ariès, P. (1962). *Centuries of childhood: A social history of family life.* New York, NY: Vintage Books.

Baumrind, D. (1966). Effects of authoritative parental control on child behavior. *Child Development, 37,* 887-907.

Baumrind, D. (1967). Child care practices anteceding three patterns of preschool behavior. *Genetic Psychology Monographs, 75,* 43-88.

Baumrind, D. (1971). Current patterns of parental authority. *Developmental Psychology Monograph, 4*(1, Pt. 2), 1-103.

Bronfenbrenner, U. (1979). *The ecology of human development: Experiments by nature and design.* Cambridge, MA: Harvard University Press.

Eyer, D. E. (1992). *Mother-infant bonding: A scientific fiction.* New Haven, CT: Yale University Press.

French, V. (1995). History of parenting: The ancient Mediterranean world. In M. H. Bornstein (Ed.), *Handbook of parenting: Biology and ecology of parenting.* (Vol. 2, pp. 263-284). Mahwah, NJ: Lawrence Erlbaum Associates.

Galinsky, E. (1987). *The six stages of parenthood.* Reading, MA: Addison-Wesley.

Gesell, A. (1928). *Infancy and human growth.* New York, NY: The Macmillan Company.

Gesell, A. & Ilg, F.L. (1943). *Infant and Child in the Culture of Today.* New York: Harper.

Kennell, J., & Klaus, M. (1984). Mother-infant bonding: Weighing the evidence. *Developmental Review, 4,* 75-82.

Klaus, M., & Kennell, J. (1976). *Maternal-infant bonding: The impact of early separation or loss on family development.* St. Louis, MO: Mosby.

Klaus, M., & Kennell, J. (1983). Parent-to-infant bonding: Setting the record straight. *Journal of Pediatrics, 102*(4), 575-576.

Lomax, E. M. R., Kagan, J., & Rosenkrantz, B. G. (1978). *Science and patterns of child care*. San Francisco, CA: W. H. Freeman and Company.

Mowder, B. A. (2005). Parent development theory: Understanding parents, parenting perceptions, and parenting behaviors. *Journal of Early Childhood and Infant Psychology, 1*, 45-64.

Mowder, B. A., Harvey, V. S., Moy, L., & Pedro, M., (1995). Parent role characteristics: Parent views and their implications for school psychologists. *Psychology in the Schools, 32*, 27 37.

Mowder, B. A., Harvey, V. S., Pedro, M., Rossen, R., & Moy, L. (1993). Parent Role Questionnaire: Psychometric characteristics. *Psychology in the Schools, 30*, 248-254.

Mowder, B. A., & Shamah, R. (2012). Parent behavior importance questionnaire-revised (PBIQ-R): Scale development and psychometric characteristics. *Journal of Child and Family Studies, 20*(3), 295-302.

Pickren, W. E., Dewsbury, D. A., & Wertheimer, M. (Eds.) (2012). *Portraits of pioneers in developmental psychology*. New York, NY: Psychology Press, Taylor & Francis Group.

Rousseau, J. J. (1762). *Émile: or on education*. (A. Bloom, Trans., Ed.). New York, NY: Basic Books.

Rousseau, J. J. (1782). *The Confessions*. New York, NY: Barnes & Noble.

Spock, B. (1946). *The common sense book of baby and child care*. New York, NY: Duell, Sloan, and Pearce.

Thompson, D., Hogan, J. D., & Clark, P. M. (2012). *Developmental psychology in historical perspective*. West Sussex, United Kingdom: Wiley-Blackwell.

Watson, J. B. (1928). *Psychological care of infant and child*. New York, NY: W. W. Norton & Company.

Watson. J.B. (1930). *Behaviorism* (Revised Edition). Chicago: University of Chicago Press.

Watson, R. (1930). I am the mother of a behaviorist's son. *The Parent's Magazine, 5*(December), 16-18, 67.

Weizmann, F., & Harris, B. (2012). Arnold Gesell: The maturationist. In W. E. Pickren, D. A. Dewsbury, & M. Wertheimer (Eds.), *Portraits of pioneers in developmental psychology*. New York, NY: Psychology Press, Taylor & Francis Group.

The Parent Development Theory: Empirical Support

Renee Krochek and Barbara A. Mowder

Abstract

The Parent Development Theory (PDT) was developed in the 1990s and is a cognitive-behavioral view of parenting that asserts that parenting is the performance of a social role. The PDT and associated parenting measures were developed concurrently so that the theory has a distinct empirical basis with a number of core ideas. First, parenting beliefs develop across an individual's lifespan, and parenting behaviors are generally consistent with one's parenting beliefs. Second, the parent role is comprised of seven parent-role characteristics that include bonding, discipline, education, general welfare and protection, responsivity, sensitivity, and negativity. Third, these characteristics change in relative importance across a child's lifespan to accommodate children's developmental needs. This article reviews the development of the PDT as well as the empirical basis for the ideas within this theory.

Key words: parent role, parent development theory, parent correlations, parent characteristics

In the early 1990s, subsequent to writing a book on the needs of at-risk and developmentally delayed infants, toddlers, and their families (i.e., Widerstrom, Mowder, & Sandall, 1991), Mowder sought a parenting theory to provide the framework for a parent-oriented book. The search for material included identifying parent-oriented measures to explore parenting related to the needs of young children. Neither a parenting theory nor a measure that was comprehensive, developmentally sensitive, psychometrically sound, and theoretically based was found. Therefore, she concurrently developed the parent development theory (PDT) and related parent assessment measures. The theory and measures informed each other's development, providing an empirical basis for the theory and a theoretical basis for the measures (Mowder, 2009).

The PDT asserts that parenting is the performance of a social role, with parents defined as those individuals who recognize, accept, and perform the role of parent. The PDT is a cognitive behavioral view of parenting and sees cognitive conceptions of the parenting role as precursors to parenting behaviors. Consistent with this view, parenting beliefs develop across an individual's lifespan and one's parenting practices will generally be consistent with his or her parenting beliefs. The parent role consists of seven parent role characteristics that include bonding, discipline, education, general welfare and protection, responsivity, sensitivity, and negativity. The relative importance or unimportance of these characteristics changes over time to accommodate children's developmental needs from infancy through adulthood. This article reviews the development of the PDT (Mowder, 2005) as well as the empirical basis for the ideas within this theory.

Empirical Basis for Seven Parent Role Characteristics

Mowder's research into the parenting role initially began with a review of the child development literature and then with focus groups representing separate sets of parents with children at various age levels (i.e., from infancy through adulthood). Based on the information collected, she determined that there are six parent role characteristics (PRCs) that constitute the parenting role, including bonding, discipline, education, general welfare and protection, responsivity, and sensitivity (Mowder, Harvey, Pedro, Rosen, & Moy, 1993). Bonding refers to showing a child love, discipline reflects setting limits and ensuring boundaries are followed, education involves educating children directly and encouraging education, general welfare and protection refers to taking care of a child's physical and safety needs, responsivity refers to attentively listening to one's child and responding appropriately, and sensitivity is learning or ascertaining an individual child's needs and matching responses to those needs (Mowder, 2005).

In order to assess the six-factor structure, Mowder developed the Parent Role Questionnaire (PRQ, (Mowder et al., 1993). This free-response and semistructured questionnaire asked respondents to describe the parenting role as well as indicate the importance and developmental sensitivity of the six identified PRCs. Results supported the importance of the six characteristics, all of which represented desirable or positive parent role characteristics.

Once the six-factor structure was mostly established by the research results, Mowder set about finding the specific parenting behaviors associated with each PRC. She developed items based on an extensive review of the literature, focus groups' responses, and responses to the PRQ. The resulting 82 items were presented to parents from two schools, and they were asked to indicate whether each behavior was important to perform using a five-point, Likert-type scale (e.g., not at all important, somewhat important, important, very important, extremely important) and how specific the item was to a parent role characteristic (e.g., bonding, discipline) (Mowder, 2000). In other words, participants indicated a level of importance and then which characteristic the behavior was most like. With regard to specifying the PRC, some items were appropriate to two, and not simply one, parent characteristic.

Based on the responses, Mowder determined that 38 parenting behaviors were important (e.g., mean rating higher than 3.0, or "important") and specific to a PRC (i.e., more than 50% of respondents indicated that the behavior was specific to a particular PRC). This provided further support for the six-factor structure (Mowder & Sanders, 2008). Based on this research, Mowder developed the Parent Behavior Importance Questionnaire (PBIQ) and Parent Behavior Frequency Questionnaire (PBFQ). The PBIQ and PBFQ measure perceptions of parenting behavior importance and frequency of performing each behavior, respectively. For the PBIQ, respondents rate the importance of each behavior using a five-point, Likert-type scale (e.g., not at all important, somewhat important), and the PBFQ uses the same five-point scale but refers to frequency instead of importance. The PBIQ instrument can be used with parents as well as, with modified directions, non-parents.

Later, Mowder recognized that the PBIQ and the PBFQ lacked appreciation of negative parenting behaviors, and she set about to incorporate a seventh characteristic, negativity, into the PRCs. Negativity refers to undesirable parenting behaviors that are associated with negative child development outcomes. Based on a consideration and study of the emotional and psychological maltreatment, verbal abuse, and verbal aggression literature, additional items were developed. Subsequently, a pool of 91 items (including positive and negative behaviors) was presented to 502 subject-matter experts (SMEs) (e.g., clinicians, graduate-level psychology students, psychologists) who, as with the PBIQ, were asked to indicate level of importance and specificity for the items. Additionally, the SMEs were asked to indicate if the behaviors were developmentally appropriate for various age groups (i.e., infant/toddler, preschooler, elementary school-aged, adolescent, late adolescent, adult) (Mowder & Shamah, 2010).

Based on the responses, 73 items were included for a revised measure determined by their importance, specificity, and developmental appropriateness. Items were included if they were important (i.e., mean importance ratings higher than 3.0, or "important"). For the negative behaviors, items were included if their mean importance rating was lower than 1.0 (i.e., the lowest level of importance, or "not at all important"). Items demonstrated specificity if the majority of respondents indicated agreement (i.e., 50% agreed the behavior corresponded to one PRC, or at least 80% agreed an item corresponded to two PRCs, with at least 30% indicating each PRC). Finally, items needed to be designated as developmentally appropriate for at least one age group for the positive parenting behaviors and as not important for any child age group for the negative items (Mowder & Shamah, 2010).

The resultant 73 items comprised the revised measures, the Parent Behavior Importance Questionnaire-Revised (PBIQ-R) and the Parent Behavior Frequency Questionnaire-Revised (PBFQ-R). More specifically, the PBIQ-R and PBFQ-R incorporated negative aspects of parenting behaviors in addition to positive parenting behaviors. Again, the PBIQ-R uses a five-point, Likert-type scale. Each of the behaviors corresponds to at least one of seven parenting scales, including bonding, discipline, education, general welfare and protection, responsivity, sensitivity, and negativity. Overall scores (e.g., Parenting Overall, Positive Parenting) as well as subscale scores (e.g., Discipline, Negativity) can be obtained (Mowder & Shamah, 2010).

Statistical analysis supported the seven parent role characteristics structure. First, internal consistency estimates were strong for the overall scale (Cronbach's *alpha* = .95) and subscales (Cronbach's *alpha* = .77 to .87). Intercorrelations among the parenting subscales were moderate to high, indicating that the subscales are related to each other and measure a coherent domain. Part-whole correlations with Pearson's r were all significant at $p < .001$ level and ranged from $r = .09$ (negativity) to $r = .81$ (education). The positive subscales were correlated with each other, but not the negative subscale, indicating that the positive PRCs are related to each other and are distinct from the negative behaviors, although there was a modest correlation between the negative and the discipline subscales. Finally, factor analysis supported the seven-factor structure of the measure. The seven-factor structure accounted for 46.84% of the variance in the PBIQ-R. While each of the seven factors did not clearly reflect each of the seven subscales of the PBIQ-R (i.e., each factor does not represent all items of each subscale), all subscales other than general welfare and protection were primarily reflected in at least one of the factors (Mowder & Shamah, 2010).

Empirical Basis for the Development of Parenting Beliefs Across the Lifespan

Based on research with Mowder's measures, results indicated that respondents of different ages hold different views regarding the importance of parenting behaviors. Notably, this is a cross-sectional and not a longitudinal design, which did not grasp the changes in an individual's perceptions over time but, rather, assessed the differences in parenting perceptions across cohorts.

In one study (Mowder, Shamah, & Zeng, 2014), 502 SMEs were asked to indicate the importance of parenting behaviors using the PBIQ-R. The respondents indicated their ages in terms of age ranges (i.e., 15-19, 20-29, 30-39, 40-49, 50-59, 60 or above). Sixty-one percent ($n = 308$) indicated ages between 20 and 29 years of age, 20% ($n = 101$) between 30 and 39, 8% ($n = 38$) between 40 and 49, 8% ($n = 38$) between 50 and 59, and 3% ($n = 15$) above 60. The SMEs only differed significantly in their importance ratings of negativity, although post-hoc analysis did not indicate where the differences reside.

A larger study explored the parenting perceptions of more than 1,700 respondents who had completed the PBIQ-R over time, including SMEs and parents (Mowder & Krochek, 2014). The ages of participants were as follows: 1% of respondents indicated that they were between ages 15 and 19 ($n = 19$), 37% between ages 20 and 29 ($n = 609$), 22% between ages 30 and 39 ($n = 365$), 22% between ages 40 and 49 ($n = 356$), 13% between ages 50 and 59 ($n = 213$), and 5% age 60 and above ($n = 87$). Results again indicated that there are significant differences in importance ratings between respondents of different ages, including bonding, discipline, education, general welfare and protection, and negativity. Post-hoc testing indicated a number of significant group differences, although all effect sizes were small. For example, for the Overall Parenting and Positive Parenting scales, the 30 to 39-year-olds rated the importance of behaviors significantly higher than the 20 to 29 and 50 to 59-year-old respondents.

Empirical Basis for the Correlation between Parenting Practices and Beliefs

The PDT asserts that parenting behaviors are generally consistent with parenting beliefs. This is a central assumption to the use of Mowder's importance rating measures (i.e., the PBIQ and the PBIQ-R), which assess parenting perceptions and do not assess frequency of parenting behaviors. Using the two early questionnaires, the Parent Behavior Importance Questionnaire and the Parent Behavior Frequency Questionnaire, Mowder and Sanders (2008) correlated the perceptions and reported frequency of parenting behaviors and found a correlation of $r = .83$. Later, Mowder and Shamah (2011) used the updated measures, the Parent Behavior Importance Questionnaire-Revised and the Parent Behavior Frequency Questionnaire-Revised, to again assess the relationship between importance perceptions and frequency of parenting behaviors. Results were again strong, indicating a strong relationship between reported parenting beliefs and reported frequency of behaviors. However, it is important to note that both measures are based on self-reporting.

Empirical Basis for the Change in Relative Importance of the Parent Role Characteristics to Accommodate Children's Developmental Needs

The developmental literature strongly supports the idea that individuals experience change as they grow and develop (e.g., John Bowlby, Erik Erikson, Sigmund Freud, Jean Piaget). That is, as children move from infancy to adulthood, their needs change based on their age. Still, few parenting theories are sensitive to children's age and how parents can promote optimal developmental outcomes through parenting that is sensitive to children's developmental needs. The PDT states that the importance of the parent role characteristics changes to accommodate children's developmental needs from infancy through adulthood. Thus, the PRCs are not static and are not performed uniformly across a child's lifespan; rather, they change in importance based on a child's developmental level and their needs at each stage.

This idea was first explored with the PRQ, which asked respondents to indicate the importance of the PRCs for different child age groups (Mowder et al., 1993). Subsequently, the PBIQ-R was used to explore the importance of specific parenting behaviors for different child age groups, including infant/toddler (birth to age 2), preschool (ages 3 to 5), elementary school (ages 13 to 18), late adolescent (ages 19 to 24) and adult children (ages 25 or older). Respondents were asked to indicate whether each parenting behavior was or was not important for each child age group (Mowder, 2009).

Later, a modified version of the PBIQ-R was developed in order to gather normative data for the measure. That is, 302 professional practitioners, including ethnically diverse individuals from varying age groups who were mostly female, were asked to indicate the importance of various parenting behaviors for different child age groups. They were asked to indicate the importance of the PBIQ-R's 73 behaviors, using a five-point, Likert-type scale, for each age group. For example, for the behavior "Being consistent establishing and following through with rules," respondents were asked to indicate an importance rating (e.g., not at all important, somewhat important) for each of the six child age groups (e.g., infant/toddler, preschooler). Results supported that parent behaviors change in importance over time and that the changes vary based on the PRCs. For example, the bonding, responsivity, and sensitivity PRCs are important during the early child age groups, increase in importance during the intermediate child age groups, and then decrease but remain relatively important into adulthood. The education, general welfare and protection, and discipline PRCs also increase in importance initially but become relatively unimportant for adult-aged children. The negativity PRC remains unimportant across a child's lifespan. Notably, all positive PRCs remain somewhat important through adulthood, indicating the importance of parenting throughout a child's life. While rated as important, the discipline PRC is the least important of all the positive PRCs across the lifespan (Krochek & Mowder, 2012; Mowder, Shamah, & Zeng, 2009).

Summary

The PDT is a cognitive behavioral view of parenting that makes a number of empirically-based assertions. For instance, parenting is comprised of a number of characteristics that include bonding, discipline, education, general welfare and protection, responsivity, sensitivity, and negativity. Individuals have parenting beliefs and perform parenting behaviors in accordance with their beliefs; these ideas change across an individual's lifespan.

The PDT and associated measures provide a number of benefits for those who work with children and parents. The theory provides a framework for understanding and exploring parenting behaviors. In relation to this benefit, practitioners have a way to conceptualize what the parent may be prioritizing in terms of parenting and to offer recommendations for adjustment in behaviors consistent with children's developmental needs. Current research into the PRCs is considering parenting in relation to child developmental outcomes. Based on these results, practitioners will have important information regarding which parenting practices are associated with positive and negative child developmental outcomes.

Practitioners can use the PDT framework to communicate with parents about their parenting behaviors; using the seven parent role characteristics, clinicians can discuss parenting behaviors in a specific and concrete way. With the understanding that parenting perceptions will be consistent with parenting behaviors, clinicians can help parents modify cognitions that are associated with negative parenting behaviors and negative child development outcomes and encourage the development of cognitions associated with the positive PRCs. The developmental data allows for guidance on how parents can adjust their parenting based on their child's developmental age.

Mowder's parenting measures also offer distinct advantages in the field of parenting. The measures are comprehensive and appreciate a wide range of parenting behaviors. They are developmentally sensitive, with norms developed for child age groups from infancy through adulthood. The measures are theoretically based and can be used with parents as well as nonparents. Use with nonparents offers the potential to preventively intervene with individuals before they are parents.

There are some limitations to the present research. First, the assertion that parenting beliefs and behaviors are consistent is based on the correlation between two self-reported measures (i.e., a measure of parenting behavior perceptions and a measure of parenting behavior frequency). Further support of this idea would be provided by direct observation of parenting behaviors after a perception measure is completed. Second, assessing for changes in parenting beliefs across an individual's lifespan is ideally achieved with a longitudinal design while the data discussed in this paper are based on a cross-sectional design. In order to further study changes in individual's parenting perceptions across time, a longitudinal design is warranted.

References

Krochek, R., & Mowder, B. A. (2012). Parenting infants: Relative importance of parenting characteristics and related behaviors. *Journal of Early Childhood and Infant Psychology, 8,* 21-34.

Mowder, B. A. (2000, March). *Parent role behaviors: Implications for school psychologists.* Paper presented at the annual meeting of the National Association of School Psychologists, New Orleans, LA.

Mowder, B. A. (2005). Parent Development Theory: Understanding parents, parenting perceptions, and parenting behaviors. *Journal of Early Childhood and Infant Psychology, 1,* 45-64.

Mowder, B. A. (2009). *Manual: Parent Behavior Importance Questionnaire-Revised (PBIQ-R)* and *Parent Behavior Frequency Questionnaire-Revised (PBFQ-R).* Manuscript in preparation.

Mowder, B. A., Harvey, V., Pedro, M., Rossen, R., & Moy, L. (1993). Parent Role Questionnaire: Psychometric qualities. *Psychology in the Schools, 30,* 205-211.

Mowder, B. A., Krochek, R. (2014). *The relationship between parenting beliefs and demographic variables.* Manuscript in preparation.

Mowder, B. A., & Sanders, M. (2008). Parent Behavior Importance and Parent Behavior Frequency Questionnaires: Psychometric characteristics. *Journal of Child and Family Studies, 17*(5), 675-688.

Mowder, B. A., & Shamah, R. (2010). Parent Behavior Importance Questionnaire-Revised: Scale development and psychometric characteristics. *Journal of Child and Family Studies, 20*(3), 295-302.

Mowder, B. A., & Shamah, R. (2011). Test-retest reliability of the Parent Behavior Importance Questionnaire-Revised and the Parent Behavior Frequency Questionnaire-Revised. *Journal of School Psychology, 48*(8), 843-854.

Mowder, B. A., Shamah, R., & Zeng, T. (2009, August). *Parenting behaviors associated with children's developmental levels.* Poster presented at the annual convention of the American Psychological Association, Toronto, Canada.

Mowder, B. A., Shamah, R., & Zeng, T. (2014). *Psychologists' perceptions of parenting behavior importance.* Manuscript in preparation.

Widerstrom, A. H., Mowder, B. A., & Sandall, S. (1991). *Newborns and infants at risk: A multidisciplinary approach to assessment and intervention.* Englewood Cliffs, NJ: Prentice-Hall.

Contemporary Parenting: The Influence of Screen Time on Parenting and Children

Alixandra Blackman and Linda Olszewski

Abstract

The aim of this article is to explore the intersection where technology meets parenting. Now more than ever, parents and children are exposed to exponentially greater amounts of screen time. Among many other changes that have resulted from rapid technological advances in our society, parent-child interactions as well as children's development are being altered by the growing dependency on screened technologies. This article outlines historically relevant research regarding the effects of screen time on children as well as contemporary parenting challenges due to the rapid changes in technology. When working with an early childhood population, an understanding of the role technology plays in a parent's and child's life as well as in the parent-child dyad is relevant.

Key words: parenting, screen time, technology, children, child development, background screen time

"Once upon a time, parenting was a seemingly simple thing: Mothers mothered; Fathers fathered" (Bornstein, 2002, p. xii). Over the years, there has been a wide array of perspectives, philosophies, suggestions, and techniques regarding how parents should raise children. Notions regarding parenting have been espoused by parents, philosophers, physicians, and psychologists who have observed the parent-child relationship through a wide variety of lenses (Bornstein, 2002). Although there have been many suggestions at the hands of experts regarding appropriate parenting, the parenting pendulum has swung between new philosophies and the simple concepts that have sustained the human race for thousands of years (Bjorklund, Yunger, & Pellegrini, 2002; Bornstein, 2002; Dorr, Rabin, & Irlen, 2002). Parents today continue to receive an overwhelming amount of advice, but now there is access to screen technology and therefore a complexity that parents in generations past did not encounter. Parents have embraced the portability and availability of today's technologies, helping to rapidly embed them into the fibers of our society. Screened devices are ever present in the lives of adults and children and are readily used by parents as a device for entertainment, a means of communication, a teacher, and even as a way to pacify and soothe children. Since technology has become deeply embedded within the daily lives of many parents and children, parents must consider the myriad of possible implications associated with screen use.

The first three years of children's lives are critical in shaping their brains' development. Early experiences help to strengthen neural pathways, which continue to impact individuals' functioning throughout their lives. These experiences have a direct impact on children's ability to learn as well as on their social and emotional abilities (National Scientific Council on the Developing Child, 2011). Neurodevelopmental research indicates that unlike other organs, which develop in utero, the human brain completes the majority of its development in response to environmental stimuli over the first 18 to 24 months of life. Stimuli that optimize the development of brain architecture include interaction with parents and other humans, manipulation of environmental elements like blocks or sand, and creative, problem-solving activities (Kaiser Family Foundation [KFF], 2005).

Although the literature regarding parenting and child development is plentiful, the introduction of rapidly enhancing technologies into the parent-child relationship is relatively new to the body of parenting research. Within the last decade the infusion of mobile technological devices such as smartphones and tablets has significantly changed the way that parents interact with their children (Taylor, 2012). Many questions remain regarding the impact of these technologies on the parent-child dyad and child development. Naturalistic observation within large cosmopolitan cities reveals this dramatic shift between parents and children. Increasingly, parents are becoming more preoccupied with their screens (e.g., a smartphone) while their young children vie for their attention. Alternatively, parents use tablets as a means of calming their children. Tablets have even been referred to as "the ultimate babysitter" due to their ability to occupy and pacify children (Silver, 2011).

This article sets out to investigate the history of research regarding technology and child development outcomes as well as the ever-expanding role technology plays within the modern parent-child relationship. The concept of screen time and the acknowledged outcomes associated with screen time (ST) are examined, as well as a phenomenon referred to as background screen time (BST). To clarify, ST can be described as one's exposure to computers, handheld devices, movies, smartphones, television (TV), video games, or other visual devices (Mayo Clinic, 2013). BST is the indirect exposure of children to their parents' direct screen time exposure. For example, this includes a TV program or video game that is played in the presence of a child who was not intended to view it (American Academy of Pediatrics [AAP], 2011). Additionally, this article discusses the importance of play between parents and children as a crucial developmental building block and the impact that technology has on play.

Historical Account of Technology in the Twentieth Century

In 300 BCE, the prolific Greek philosopher Plato made the following assertion about entertaining children:

[A] young person cannot judge what is allegorical and what is literal; anything that he receives into his mind at that age is likely to become indelible and unalterable; and therefore it is most important that the tales which the young first hear should be models of virtuous thoughts. (Sigler, 1997, p. 6)

Plato's concerns about children's exposure to potentially inappropriate forms of entertainment were echoed throughout history. These concerns became particularly strong amongst child advocates in the 20th century (Dorr et al., 2002). It was during this time that parents, social commentators, and social scientists alike worried that comic books, movies, radio programs, and television would be harmful to children (Luke, 1990; Wartella & Reeves, 1985). In the 1930s, as film became available to the general public, there was great concern regarding the influence of popular films on children's attitudes, emotions, and social conduct. Motivated by public concern, The Payne Fund Studies set out to address the potentially negative effects of film content on young people (Dworkin, 1970). Researchers found the expected attitudinal effects. Among other findings, the study found that movie watchers were less cooperative, had lower conduct grades, were rated lower in reputation by their teachers and classmates, and did poorer in school. These effects were positively correlated with film exposure, and the effects persisted over time. However, the general public largely ignored the results of these studies. Jowett, Jarvie, and Fuller (1996) believe that the film industry manipulated the decreased public interest in the research findings. Regardless, these studies still hold relevance today, as popular movies continue to be a part of young people's media experiences and concerns persist about their effects (Dorr et al.).

Shortly after the popularity of films worked its way into American culture, the next wave of technology made its way into American homes: the television. The television was introduced to America in 1939 at the World's Fair in New York, and by 1945, 7,000 homes across America owned working televisions (Tamazashvili, 2007). Americans were quickly taken by this convenient device that provided endless hours of entertainment, and by the 1950s televisions were commonplace within American households (Dorr et al.). In 1954, Maccoby reported that all other family life virtually stopped when the television was on. Similar to the concerns raised by the popularity of film, concerns regarding the negative effects of television on children have persisted since its inception. Research began in the 1960s and was fueled by Bandura's Social Learning Theory (1963), which demonstrated that children learn through observation. Media studies of the 1960s found that young children learned and reproduced specific acts of aggression that they observed on film (Lovaas, 1961). More specifically, a study found that groups of children who observed either a filmed adult aggressive model or a live adult aggressive model displayed equal amounts of aggression (Bandura, Ross, & Ross, 1963). Research in the 1960s also indicated that if a child aged 3 to 6 observed someone on film being rewarded for any sort of behavior, even aggressive behavior, it increased their chances of imitating the behavior. Likewise, if they viewed a televised model being punished for aggressive behavior, children aged 3 to 6 were less likely to imitate the action (Bandura, 1965).

In the 1970s, research established the power that television had on influencing the behavior of young children. First, research confirmed television's ability to teach aggressive behavior through modeling (Murray, 1972), and second, with the arrival of Sesame Street, research demonstrated that TV could be a powerful teacher of academic and social skills. These efforts ushered in a period that established the need for creating effective educational programs for children. Five-year-olds who watched Sesame Street in the presence of toys paid half as much attention to the TV screen as did 5-year-olds who watched the same program without toys. However, comprehension was the same for both groups, suggesting that young children monitor the audio track of television programs for cues indicating content that interests them and distribute their visual attention strategically (Lorch, Anderson, & Levin, 1979). Research of this decade also found that children who watched more television at ages 3, 4, and 5 had lower grades and were rated as less sociable by their peers at age 6 (Burton, Calonico, & McSeveny, 1979).

The research of the 1980s continued to explore the effects of media on children (Pearl, Bouthilet, & Lazar, 1982). A study indicated that imaginative play increased after children saw either a low action/low violence program or no television, but decreased after a high action/high violence program. Aggressive behavior increased after viewing a high action/high violence or high action/low violence program (Huston-Stein, Fox, Greer, Watkins, & Whitaker, 1981). Preschoolers who had behavior problems in school watched more television than children who did not have behavior problems in school; these aggressive children also specifically watched more violent, action-adventure programs and fewer prosocial programs (Singer & Singer, 1980). A study by Gadberry (1980) found that reducing young children's television time might increase their scores on IQ and Matching Familiar Figures tests as well as the time they spent reading.

In the 1970s, American children also gained another form of entertainment with the introduction of the first household video game console. The popularity of video games exploded in the 1980s and they continue to be popular today. While parents' concerns regarding movies and television have received a significant amount of attention, the controversy regarding video games has been more ardent, even leading to a Supreme Court case ruling in favor of the video game industry's right to free speech (*Brown v. Entertainment Merchants Association*, 2011). The popularity of violent video games has been blamed for tragic events such as increases in bullying, school shootings, and violence toward women. This debate over violent video games can be traced back to the 1970s with the release of a game called Death Race. Critics believed the game encouraged violent acts in children and the controversy resulted in protestors dragging Death Race machines out of arcades and burning them in parking lots across America until production of the game ceased (Ferguson, Rueda, Cruz, Ferguson, & Fritz, 2008).

The fervor of video game critics has not waned over the years, and in 1993 public outcry following the releases of violent video games Mortal Kombat and Night Trap influenced Congress to put pressure on the video game industry to institute the Entertainment Software Rating Board (ESRB) to create an age-appropriate rating system for video games ("Critics Zap Video Games," 1994). While this seemed to quell the public for some time, a more recent study by the Pew Research Center in 2008 found that 50% of boys and 14% of girls aged 12-17 listed a game with "Mature" or "Adults Only" ratings in their current top three favorite games (Lenhart et al., 2008). In 2005 the American Psychological Association (APA) called for the reduction of violence in video games marketed to youth because of possible links between video games and aggression toward women (APA, 2005). Defenders of violent video games argue that research has failed to show a causal link between video games and real-world violence. They state that if video games do cause violence, then one would expect juvenile violent crime to increase as more youth play violent video games. However, the arrest rate for juvenile violent crimes has fallen 49.3% between 1995 and 2008, while video game sales have quadrupled in the same period (Federal Bureau of Investigation [FBI], 2009). In 2011, Kids & Gaming reported that 91% of children ages 2-17 play video games, and within the last few years, gaming for children ages 2-5 has increased the most. Currently, 76% of parents report that they place time limits on children's video game playing (Entertainment Software Association, 2013).

"An interdisciplinary approach dominated the investigation of media effects on young children during the 1990s" (Schmidt et al., 2005, p. 6). Individuals from a variety of fields, including communication, education, medicine, psychology, and public health, applied their approaches to research in this field (*Brown v. Entertainment Merchants Association*, 2011), which increased our spectrum of understanding of children's viewing habits. Researchers found that children's comprehension of TV is higher when they are engaged, and their attention is maximized if information is provided in the auditory and visual modes (Lorch & Castle, 1997;

Rolandelli, Wright, Huston, & Eakins, 1991). Older children have a more sophisticated understanding of the material presented on the TV. Three-year-olds often mistake TV images for real characters and situations that reside within the TV set, while 4-year-olds can recognize televised images as pictorial representations (Flavell & Flavell, 1990). Two-year-olds have difficulty using information from a televised event to understand a real-life situation (Troseth & DeLoache, 1998). Additionally, the ability of children between the ages of 12-18 months to learn from televised images lags behind their ability to learn from live, observed events (Barr & Hayne, 1999).

Sesame Street was studied extensively, and research found that viewing it was beneficial to children's vocabulary development. Children who spent more time viewing *Sesame Street* achieved higher scores on a picture test of vocabulary, regardless of parental education, family size, gender, and parental attitudes (Rice, Huston, Truglio, & Wright, 1990). A longitudinal study of children's television use found that children tend to watch adult television programs in the presence of their parents and child programs without their parents present (St. Peters, Fitch, Huston, Wright, & Eakins, 1991). The more time children spent co-viewing with parents, the less time they spent watching educational programs (Taras, Sallis, Nader, & Nelson, 1990). Viewing frightening television, even programming deemed appropriate for preschoolers, raised children's heart rates and caused symptoms of post-traumatic stress disorder (PTSD) that lasted at least a month (Groer & Howell, 1990).

By the end of the 20th century, Americans' screen exposure increased yet again as computer technology reached the general public. At that time, half or more of American homes with children ages 2 to 18 had Internet access, personal computers, and video game consoles (Roberts, Foehr, Rideout, & Brodie, 1999). Between 1999 and 2000, households with Internet access across America grew from 41% to 52% (Woodard & Gridina, 2000). Children's media-rich environments continued to expand. According to the Media in the Home 2000 survey, in homes with children ages 2-17, 70%

owned a computer, 68% owned video games, and 52% had online access; 98% of homes had at least one television, 97% owned a VCR, and 78% had a subscription to basic cable. Media also began to permeate many children's bedrooms: Among 8- to 16-year olds, 20% had a computer in their bedroom, of which 54% had Internet access (Woodard & Gridina, 2000).

Within a 70-year span, technology has made its way into the American household, shaping the way in which entertainment and information are disseminated to families. As the 21st century continues to progress, the technological advances continue to shift dramatically, offering individuals portability and mobility with devices. These technologies can travel with us in our backpacks, pockets, and purses. Within the last decade, the extraordinary popularity of smartphones and tablets boomed, providing people with unlimited information, entertainment, and the ability to conduct business at any time and in any place. While they have provided a great deal of luxury and simplicity, they also have created a new way for parents and children to engage and interact.

Contemporary Screen Time Research

The American Academy of Pediatrics (AAP) has issued a policy statement recommending that infants and children under age 2 should avoid television and other entertainment media. They also recommend that children over the age of 2 should be limited to a maximum of two hours of high-quality educational programming per day (AAP, 2001). The AAP cited research demonstrating adverse effects of screen time (ST) on the health and developmental outcomes in children ages 2 and younger. The AAP informs parents that children's brains develop rapidly during these first years, and young children learn best by interacting with people, not screens. However, research examining media use by very young children has indicated that the vast majority of parents have never heard of these recommendations and continue to allow and even encourage their very young children to use screened media (Rideout,

2013; Rideout, Vandewater, & Wartella, 2003). A later study by Funk, Brouwer, Curtiss, and McBroom (2009) suggested that only 34% of parents with children under the age of 5 are even aware of the AAP recommendations for screen time.

Despite the AAP's recommendations, parents are introducing their children to screen time at very young ages. A 2004 report found that infants were being shown videos at a mean age of 6.1 months and television at a mean age of 9.8 months for an average of about two hours daily (Weber & Singer, 2004). A 2005 report revealed that children become autonomous users of computers by 3.5 years of age (Calvert, Rideout, Woolard, Barr, & Strouse, 2005). The Zero to Six study (Rideout et al., 2003) found that 74% of children under the age of 2 have watched television and 59% watch television on a typical day for an average of two hours and five minutes. Thirty percent of children ages 0 to 3 and 43% of children 4 to 6 have televisions in their bedrooms. Those with screens in their bedrooms use media for more time each day, and children in "heavy television" homes read less and learn to read later than those in other homes. Despite the data, more parents believe that television "mostly helps" rather than "mostly hurts" their children's learning (43% vs. 27%) (Rideout et al.).

Many parents view TV as a peacekeeper and a safe activity for their children while they are doing household chores, getting ready for work, or preparing dinner (Rideout & Hamel, 2006). In 2007, Sigman estimated that children now spend more time at home alone in front of screens than doing anything else. Researchers have even revealed that a child is the target of media programming and can engage with various forms of media for up to eight hours per day starting at the age of 4 months (Council On Communications and Media, 2011; Roberts, Foehr, & Rideout 2006; Vandewater, Park, Huang, & Wartella, 2005; Zimmerman, Christakis, & Meltzoff, 2007). Educational DVDs/videos, television programs, and even entire cable networks are geared toward children (AAP, 2011). This indicates that despite the warning from the AAP, children under the age of

2 are frequently engaging in ST. Not only are children exposed to screens at this young age, but many parents are also giving their children the freedom to choose what they watch, specifically for toddlers with TVs in their bedrooms (Rideout et al., 2003).

Due to the rapid growth of the technology sector within such a short period of time, research is only beginning to catch up, offering statistics and potential outcomes associated with ST. While the majority of studies conducted in the arena of ST only examine one form of media at a time, such as television or video games, a 2013 study reveals that the average 8- to 10-year-old spends nearly eight hours per day with different media, and older children and teens spend more than 11 hours per day with media. Furthermore, children who have a TV in their bedroom are exposed to even more ST. About 75% of 12- to 17-year-olds own cell phones, and nearly all teenagers use text messaging (AAP, 2013).

Although the controversy regarding children's TV exposure has leaned toward exposing the negatives associated with ST, research has indicated some benefits as well. One study found that 1-year-olds avoided an object after they watched an actress react negatively to it on video, suggesting that infants can apply emotional reactions seen on television to guide their own behavior (Mumme & Fernald, 2003). Depending upon the content of the TV programming, the ability to apply emotional reactions viewed on a screen may lead to positive or negative behavioral effects for young children.

Language development in the context of TV is a controversial area, which research has associated with both positive and negative effects. Linebarger and Walker (2005) indicated the importance of TV program content and found potential benefits, such as increased vocabulary growth, with interactive programs that provide a narrative structure, such as *Arthur, Blue's Clues, Clifford, Dora the Explorer,* and *Dragon Tales*. Children who regularly watched Blue's Clues scored higher on standardized measures of problem solving and flexible thinking than children who did not watch *Blue's*

Clues, even though both groups of children had scored equivalently on a pre-test prior to *Blue's Clues* exposure (Anderson et al., 2000). Educational TV viewing at 2 and 3 years of age predicted school readiness among low- to moderate-income children (Wright et al., 2001). Anderson, Huston, Schmitt, Linebarger, and Wright (2001) conducted a longitudinal study across the United States, which found that preschoolers who viewed educational TV programs had higher grades and read more books in high school; however, among girls, viewing violent programs in preschool was associated with lower high school grades. On the contrary, a longitudinal analysis, the National Longitudinal Survey of Youth-Child, revealed that each one-hour increase in TV viewing prior to the age of 3 negatively affects cognitive and language performance at the age of 6 (Baker, Keck, Mott, & Quinlan, 1993; Zimmerman & Christakis, 2005). Audible TV has also been associated with decreased vocalizations in infants (Christakis et al., 2009). A Japanese study linked high amounts of television viewing with less talking and delayed speech development in infants and young children (Tinamura, Okuma, & Kyoshima, 2007). A contradictory study revealed that viewing TV in infancy does not seem to be associated with language or visual motor skills at 3 years of age (Schmidt, Rich, Rifas-Shiman, Oken, & Taveras, 2009).

TV exposure has also been associated with increased attention problems. Data from the National Longitudinal Survey of Youth indicated that TV viewing at age 1 and 3 was associated with parental reports of attention disorder symptoms at age 7. For every additional 2.9 hours of TV viewed per week at age 1, a child was 28% more likely to exhibit attention disorder symptoms at age 7 (Christakis, Zimmerman, DiGiuseppe, & McCarty, 2004). Christakis (2011) stated that fast-paced cartoons have been correlated with attention problems; however, these effects on attention are temporary. While the effects are temporary, fast-paced cartoons are able to impact children's executive functioning abilities and over time may indeed have a profound impact on children's cognitive and social-emotional development (Christakis, 2011; Lillard & Peterson, 2011). Early exposure to media is also a predictor of aggression in later childhood (AAP, 1999; AAP, 2011; Rich, 2007).

Many studies support a correlation between TV viewing and aggressive behavior in children over the age of 6; however, there is little research on the effects on children between the ages of 0-6, who are at a very critical period in development (Mistry, Minkovitz, Strobino, & Borzekowski, 2007; Thakkar, Garrison, & Christakis, 2006). TV viewing has also been found to increase the risk for both psychological and academic problems in children. Studies reveal that the more a child is viewing TV, the greater their risk for psychological difficulties, difficulties with peer relationships, poor homework completion, negative attitudes toward school, poor academic achievement, and long-term academic failure (Johnson, Brook, Cohen, & Kasen, 2007; Page, Cooper, Griew, & Jago, 2010). Some studies suggest that early exposure to TV is not only linked to lower math and school achievements, but also to victimization by classmates and reduced physical activity in later childhood (Landhuis, Poulton, Welch, & Hancox, 2008; Pagani, Fitzpatrick, Barnett, & Dubow, 2010).

Research regarding the effects of video games on children's minds has yielded positive and negative outcomes. Prot, McDonald, Anderson, and Gentile (2012) outlined the main research findings of the positive and negative effects of video games on players. Research has found that action games improve a range of visuospatial skills, educational games successfully teach specific knowledge and skills, exercise games can improve physical activity levels, and prosocial games increase empathy and helping and may decrease aggression (Achtman, Green, & Bavelier, 2008; Greitemeyer & Osswald, 2010; Murphy, Penuel, Means, Korbak, & Whaley, 2002; Rhodes, Warburton, & Bredin, 2009; Sestir & Bartholow, 2010). On the contrary, violent games have been shown to increase aggressive behaviors, feelings, and thoughts; desensitize players to violence; and decrease empathy and helping. Video game play has been negatively related to school performance and may exacerbate attention problems, and some players have been shown to become addicted to video games (Anderson, Gentile, & Buckley, 2007; Anderson et al., 2010; Bartholow, Sestir, & Davis, 2005; Bushman & Anderson, 2009; Carnagey, Anderson, & Bushman, 2007; Gentile, 2009; Swing, Gentile, Anderson, & Walsh, 2010). With this in mind, the content of a video game is an essential factor in contributing to potential negative outcomes.

Today's child typically lives in an environment where parents own an average of four digital devices each (Rideout, 2013). On average, 83% of American households own HDTVs, 80% own Internet-connected computers, 65% own smartphones, 49% own digital recorders, and 46% own gaming consoles (AAP, 1999; Nielsen Report, 2013; Rideout, Foehr, & Roberts, 2010). A 2005 report reveals that children become autonomous users of computers by 3.5 years of age (Calvert et al., 2005), and an international survey of 2,200 mothers conducted by Environment and Human Health, Inc. (Wargo et. al., 2012) found that more children between the ages of 2 through 5 could play with a smartphone application than could tie their shoelaces. Within the last decade, there has been an explosion of electronic media that primarily targets children under the age of 2 and their parents. Contrary to the AAP recommendations, parents are utilizing these applications and electronic devices as a means of educating and entertaining their children. Smartphones, tablets, computers, and other media devices are now portable, and they have transformed viewing time into something that is constantly available. These technological devices serve as temptation for parents, who want to constantly entertain and soothe their babies and toddlers (Wooldridge, 2010). Some time ago, John Watson (1928) encouraged parents to present their infants with an object to become attached to since, in his view, children should not become too attached to a caregiver. Unfortunately, with the popularity and accessibility of technological devices, Watson's wish seems to be beginning to come true.

An article by De Lacey (2012), published in the United Kingdom, stated this matter simply: "Mothers now prefer handing over smartphones rather than dummies [pacifiers] to comfort crying babies." A survey by the Daily Mail (De Lacey) indicated that one in four mothers is using smartphones to calm children over the use of a pacifier. Rideout and Hamel (2006) have indicated that American parents are similarly using technology. The number one reason parents cite for why their very young children use screen media is to release them from minding the child in order to accomplish other tasks (Rideout & Hamel, 2006). The use of screen media is further reported to relieve parental guilt for lack of face-to-face interaction (Garrison & Christakis, 2005). This is concerning for many reasons, but particularly for a child's ability to self-soothe and self-regulate. Parents who assist an infant in the first few months with arousal control and moderation of sensory input find self-regulation developing into impulse control and greater compliance in the child's second year of life (Kopp, 1982). If children are more commonly being soothed by staring at a screen, as opposed to traditional methods such as sucking on a pacifier or engaging in other self-soothing activities, how will this impact a child's future ability to self-regulate their behaviors and emotions when faced with overwhelming or overstimulating situations? Will this increase inattention, hyperactivity, or perhaps anxiety within children? There are many questions that remain unanswered.

Background Screen Time

A sensitive and stimulating home is positively associated with academics, cognition, language, and social competence in children. Among the most important influences in development are social interactions with family, peers, teachers, and others (National Institute of Child Health and Human Development [NICHD], 2003). Background screen time (BST) may contribute to a reduction in these social interactions. The AAP (2011) addresses the adverse effects of BST and reports that BST negatively impacts a child because it restricts a parent from engaging with their child in a meaningful way (Hart & Risley, 1995). BST has the direct effect of distracting a child and the indirect effect of taking parents' attention away from children. Researchers believe that although infants and toddlers pay low levels of overt attention to adult programs that they cannot understand, parents are distracted when the TV is on, and this decreases parent-child interactions (Anderson & Evans, 2001; Kirkorian, Pempek, Murphy, Schmidt, & Anderson, 2009; Rideout & Hamel, 2006; Schmidt, Pempek, Kirkorian, Lund, & Anderson, 2008).

The quality of parent-child relationships during early childhood has important implications for the emergence of social competence and social relations when children enter school. Sensitive and responsive parenting behaviors place children on a developmental trajectory for increased competence. Parents who are consistent in their disciplinary practices and respond sensitively to the needs of their toddlers have children who internalize their standards, are securely attached, demonstrate cognitive competence, and exhibit fewer behavior problems during preschool and middle childhood (Grusec & Goodnow, 1994; Kochanska, 1995). In studies of attachment, mothers of secure children provide more support and assistance to their children during interactional tasks than mothers of insecurely attached children. Mothers who are rated as more affectionate, responsive, and supportive have been shown to be more likely to have toddlers with a secure attachment style (Bates, Maslin, & Frankel, 1985; Pastor, 1981). On the contrary, parents of insecurely attached children display less support and a lower quality of assistance to their children during problem-solving tasks than mothers of securely attached children (Fagot, Gauvain, & Kavanagh, 1996). The high rates of screen time use may impact attachment, and a report from the United Kingdom claims, "television alone is displacing the parental role, eclipsing by a factor of five or ten the time parents spend actively engaging with children" (Sigman, 2009, p. 15).

Currently, it is estimated that two-thirds of children under the age of 6 are exposed to background media at least half of their waking hours (Lapierre, Piotrowski, & Linebarger, 2012). A 2014 study determined that young children under the age of 2 frequently watch background media that has age-inappropriate content or that has not been turned on for them to watch (Tomopoulos et al., 2014). Many families have reported that they have a television on at least six hours per day or that a television is "always on" as background noise (Roberts & Foehr, 2004). Thirty-nine percent of families with infants and young children have a television on constantly (Vandewater et al., 2005). Sixty-one percent of parents have an adult television program on while a child is in the room some of the time, while 29% of parents report that they do this all or most of the time (Rideout & Hamel, 2006). A 2012 study by Lapierre et al. found that the average child in the United States is exposed to four hours of background TV per day. They determined that the youngest children, between 8 and 24 months, are exposed to even more background TV, with an average of 5.5 hours per day. Additionally, the research determined that African American children, children from low-income families, children living in single-parent households, and children of parents with less formal education were exposed to even higher levels of background television per day. These children are also more likely to live in homes where traditional foreground ST exposure plays a greater role during the day (Gentile & Walsh, 2002; Huston & Bentley, 2010; Lee, Bartolic, & Vandewater, 2009).

Children's emotional growth is directly related to parenting behaviors and meaningful interactions between parents and children. In a study which considered the impact that background TV has on the quantity and quality of parent-child interactions, researchers found that background TV reduced overall interactions due to a reduction in parents' active engagement (Kirkorian et al., 2009). Furthermore, parents' TV viewing can result in poor relationships between parents and children (Vandewater et al.,

2006). Manganello and Taylor (2009) found that BST exposure in children under the age of 3 increased the risk that children would behave aggressively. They suggested that 3-year-old children who are exposed to more than two hours of TV per day, including BST, are at a heightened risk for conduct problems. Similarly, BST also affects sibling relationships. When a sibling is distracted by television, the interaction between siblings is undermined (Anderson & Evans, 2001; Kirkorian et al., 2009).

The results of many studies suggest that background media may interfere with cognitive processing, memory, and reading comprehension (Armstrong & Greenberg, 1990; Gottfried, 1984; Schmidt et al., 2008; Vandewater et al., 2005). These studies support the notion that children rely on their caregiver's communication as a foundation for their language development (Christakis et al., 2009; Hoff & Naigles, 2002). Studies indicate that parents compromise the quality of their children's language when they are distracted by television, because their attention is drawn away from children (Lavigne, Hanson, Pempeck, Kirkorian, & Anderson, 2011; Pempek, Kirkorian, & Anderson, 2010; Zimmerman et al., 2009). Background media also has an influence on children's academic abilities, specifically their reading ability. The more background media children are exposed to, the less likely that they will be read to (Rideout & Hamel, 2006), and being read to has been linked to developing early literacy skills. BST has an impact on children's ability to focus and pay attention as well. If children are trying to do homework or play with a television on in the background, they will orient to changes on the screen and become distracted from what they are doing, shifting their attention away from a self-directed activity and toward the flash of light of an image change on the TV (DeGaetano, 2004). A study by Armstrong, Bolarsky, and Mares (1991), which investigated the effects of background television on cognitive performance, found a significant deleterious effect of background television when controlling for ability and motivation. Additionally, the content of the background television played a role, with background commercials resulting in more consistent negative effects than did a television drama.

While background media has detrimental effects on various aspects of children's development, a Portuguese study also found that increased background media leads to increased direct screen time for children. This study found that parental TV-viewing time was strongly associated with child weekday and weekend TV-viewing time. Maternal TV-viewing time was a stronger predictor of child TV-viewing time than paternal TV-viewing time. Additionally, access to electronic devices increased the likelihood that children would spend greater than one hour using combined media devices on weekdays and weekends. This study also determined that the number of TVs and electronic devices in a household were also associated with the frequency of screen time for parents and their children (Jago et al., 2012). A 1999 report (Roberts et al.) stated that a majority (63%) of 2- to 7-year-old children were co-viewing with their parents in the evening, and as children got older they were more likely to view alone, less likely to view with parents, and somewhat less likely to view with siblings. While BST exposure has been linked to a variety of relational and cognitive detriments, there is research that provides parents with a way to mediate these negative effects. Mendelsohn et al. (2010) found that if parents interact with their children and communicate about what they are seeing on the screen, this can lessen the negative effects of BST. This finding underlines how essential the line of communication is to the health of the parent-child dyad and exemplifies one important way in which parents and children can continue to be media consumers while not missing opportunities to interact with one another.

The Impact of Technology on Play

Piaget (1932) considered play to be one of the foremost avenues of children's cognitive development. He believed that play provides children with opportunities to construct knowledge about the world through interaction with objects in the environment. Representational skills, memory, concepts, problem solving, perspective taking, language skills, and creativity are learned through play (Davidson, 1998; Singer, Singer, Plaskon, & Schweder, 2003). Play is a form of early communication, establishing shared meaning between parent and child (McCune, 1992). Play is a time for adults to scaffold children's language abilities as the play content centers on the child's explorations and interests. This allows a parent to secure their child's attention and enhances mutual communication between them (Bakeman & Adamson, 1984; Bruner, 1975; McArthur & Adamson, 1996; Tomasello & Farrar, 1986). Maternal responsiveness has been directly related to joint attention in early language acquisition because mothers are focusing on the same interests as their children. Background noise in the home, mainly from televisions, is negatively related to maternal responsiveness, possibly because background noise interferes with parent verbal stimulation, thereby reducing contingent responsiveness to the child (Corapci & Wachs, 2000). Play is an essential element in children's development and a reduction in parent's play with children, perhaps caused by ST or BST, may influence many early developmental processes, particularly the development of language, reading, and literacy (Davidson, 1998; Zigler, Singer, & Bishop-Josef, 2004).

The mere presence of parents, although certainly important, does not produce optimum conditions for development. Rather, children flourish when parents are actively involved in their play (Kirkorian et al., 2009). An experiment by Slade (1987) found that toddlers exhibited substantially longer play episodes and more sophisticated play when mothers made suggestions and were physically involved compared to when mothers only passively commented on child-initiated verbal interactions. A 2008 study reported that a substantial proportion of very young children's solitary toy play and play with parents occurs in the presence of television (Masur & Flynn, 2008). Research has found that when the TV is on, even if the program is not intended for their viewing, children play and interact less with adults, perhaps because the adult's attention is focused on the TV program and not on their child, or perhaps background noise interferes with parent-child interactions (Kirkorian et al., 2009).

Background television can be quite disruptive to young children's play. Evans (2003) and Kirkorian (2004) found that when the TV is on, children's play episodes are shorter, with less focused attention, and there are fewer parent-child exchanges. A study, which observed children between the ages of 1 and 3 during a one-hour home play session where the television was on in the background for half the time, found that, even with minimal and sporadic viewing by the children, play with toys was significantly reduced, as was focused attention during play (Schmidt et al., 2008). A correlational study of children 11 to 18 months of age found that in a context in which the TV was turned off some of the infants were not used to the quiet. This prompted researchers to question whether parent-infant interactions in the absence of background television represent a "normal" play context in the home of today's infants (Masur & Flynn, 2008).

Not only are ST and BST having an impact on children's play, but also many of the toys of today are electronic devices in some form. In the last several years, traditional toys have been increasingly replaced as more shelf space is given to electronic toys, and the electronic toys have become the most popular and desired by children (Business Wire, 2007; Ritchel & Stone, 2007; Wall, 2006). For example, there are now laptop computers for infants and toddlers, electronic talking books, animated stuffed animals and dolls, digital cameras for little hands, and battery-driven materials of every kind, including infant rattles. Parents and early childhood educators must now actively search for toys and materials that do not flash lights, speak, or direct children's play by preprogrammed, technical scripts (Wooldridge, 2010).

Many parents view these toys as educational and beneficial for their young children. Infancy, it would seem for some, is considered primarily a period for teaching in the academic sense (Garrison & Christakis, 2005). A 2005 Kaiser Family Foundation report reviewed electronic products for children from birth to 6 years from five major retailers (Garrison & Christakis). A Baby Einstein video aimed at infants as young as 1 month claimed to create "learning opportunities" (Wooldridge, 2010, p. 14). A Nick Jr. video for 3-month-olds claimed to be "specifically designed for babies' social, emotional, cognitive, and physical development" (Wooldridge, p. 14). The parent feedback found in the report suggests that parents believe the educational claims of such products: "there is so much education in this video" (Wooldridge, p. 15); "he will come away…with more synapses in his brain than had he not watched" (Wooldridge, p. 15). A more recent study affirmed this finding and revealed that parents do, indeed, believe the educational claims made on toy packaging (Wong et al., 2008). In 2007, there were 550 new software titles aimed at children (Buckleitner, 2008). In 2006, educational products for babies alone represented a $20 billion industry in U.S. dollars (Knowledge@Wharton, 2007). Baby Einstein videos alone, marketed specifically for infants under 1 year of age, earned $250 million in annual revenue by 2006, 10 years following its creation (Guernsey, 2007; Wooldridge).

The issue remains that there is a lack of research regarding the educational benefits of such toys. Brain imaging studies have found that the developing brain of an infant responds differently to live versus televised stimuli than does an adult brain. Two-dimensional images on a screen present a "different reality in the observer's brain compared to the live setting and thus does not merely attenuate brain responses of visual stimuli" (Shimada & Hiraki, 2006, p. 937; Wooldridge, 2010). Children under 30 months are thought to suffer a "video deficit," which means that they are able to learn from live human models, but not from screens (Anderson & Pempek, 2005; Barr & Hayne, 1999; Troseth & DeLoache, 1998). In 2005, Garrison and Christakis extended their research beyond television to include all screen technology designed as learning tools for very young children and concluded that "preliminary research indicates that the various media may be less effective in educating very young children than are other activities that they may well be displacing – such as one-on-one parental interaction" (p. 33). There is also concern that interactions with new technologies do not afford a child the opportunity to be creative, which has been observed to be fundamental to a child's ability to learn (Resnick, 2006).

Luckin, Connolly, Plowman, and Airey (2003) stated that interactive media has the potential to provide scaffolding support to children, because they can act in a "collaborative partnership role" (p. 166). Studies of preschool children's interactions with technology-enhanced toys indicate that these toys initially foster exploration of the technological features of the toy rather than encourage practice or pretend play, especially for children who have not had previous exposure to these types of toys. However, as play continues, children's existing play schemas often emerge. For example, toys may be used in routine, familiar actions such as "cooking dinner" or "going to sleep" (Bergen, 2007).

On the contrary, a study by Wooldridge (2010) found that using electronic toys with toddlers might be detrimental to the quality of parent-child interaction and that they fail to assist the early learning goals that parents may have for their children. She found that a strong majority of parents consider early learning as the primary purpose of their children's play. When using electronic toys versus traditional toys, mothers were less responsive, less encouraging, and less instructive. Specifically, mothers were significantly more instructive with traditional toys than with electronic toys. The study found that mothers lacked engagement in pretend play with their child when using electronic toys. Pretend play in particular is the forum in which young children develop problem-solving, divergent thinking, alternative coping strategies, adaptive perspective-taking, as well as more complex emotional expressions (Russ, 2004). It is the major play form that promotes and supports the development of self-regulation and social competency (Elias & Berk, 2002). Given the weight of evidence about the critical value of pretend play in children's healthy development, it is important that parents are informed that traditional, non-electronic toys are more likely to inspire engagement and instruction in pretend play. Parents model and mediate the symbolic use of toys and actions in pretend scenarios and teach their children how to do this. The toddler period is particularly critical as make-believe starts in the second year in rich parent-toddler interaction (Berk, 2010; Wooldridge, 2010). Research indicates that the technological sophistication of electronic toys may fail to replicate the parents' role in the development of make-believe play and, likely, in the child's overall development (Wooldridge).

Recommendations

After reviewing the literature on ST and BST, it is clear that parents today rely heavily on technology to help perform otherwise typical parent roles such as educating and calming a child. Parents must remember that, while technology provides us with convenience and comfort in the short-term, overreliance on these devices may heed consequences in the lives of children and parents alike.

With the creative and continuous innovation within the field of technology, there has been an increase in device options in a relatively short amount of time. It is evident that both content and limits for children's ST exposure are certainly important. It is also important for parents to limit their own ST while in the presence of their children, particularly during moments of play.

It is important for parents to be aware of the AAP recommendations for children under the age of 2, particularly because there are many unknowns regarding the impact of overexposure to screened technologies on a child's neurological development. The AAP recommends that parents establish "screen-free" zones at home by making sure that there are no televisions, computers, or video games in children's bedrooms and by turning off the TV during dinner; that parents limit screen time to two hours per day for children over the age of 2; and that they offer educational media in non-electronic formats such as books, newspapers, and board games. Parents should watch television with their children and help kids put content into context. It is also encouraged that children spend time playing outdoors, reading, and using their imaginations in free play.

Conclusion

Parents and children alike are distracted by the appeal of technology, spending a significant amount of time staring at screens, engaged in a virtual reality. The overlap between our real and virtual worlds is continually increasing as these devices become embedded in the daily lives of parents and children; however, there are consequences for this overreliance on technology. Determining children's access and exposure to technology is an extraordinarily important role entrusted to parents. Research has depicted that parents' active engagement with their children as well as their choice of an appropriate media diet for their children plays a significant role in child development.

Highlights from Contemporary Parenting:
The Influence of Screen Time on Parenting and Children

- The American Academy of Pediatrics (AAP) recommends that TV and other entertainment media should be avoided for infants and children under the age of 2.
- The AAP further recommends that children over the age of 2 should be limited to a maximum of two hours of high-quality educational programming per day.
- The vast majority of parents has never heard the recommendations from the AAP and encourages their very young children to use screened media.
- The number one reason parents cite for why they allow their very young children to use screened media is to release them from minding their children in order to accomplish other tasks.
- Young children learn best by interacting with people, not screens.
- Increased screen time (ST) exposure in children has been linked to delayed language acquisition, reduction in literacy, attention problems, behavioral problems, and academic difficulties.
- The content of children's ST plays a role as well. Interactive programs that provide a narrative structure (e.g., Blue's Clues) have been linked to positive educational and developmental outcomes, while violent and age inappropriate content has been linked to aggression and decreased academic achievement.
- Increased background screen time (BST) has been linked to a reduction in parent-child interactions and parents' active engagement with their children; an increased risk of aggressive behavior in children under the age of 3; and an interference with cognitive processing, memory, and reading comprehension.
- BST is disruptive to young children's play, causing shorter play episodes, less focused attention, and fewer parent-child exchanges.
- When playing with electronic vs. traditional toys, mothers were less responsive, less encouraging, and less instructive.

Tips:

- Adhere to the AAP recommendations in terms of both content and exposure.
- Mediate the negative effects of BST by communicating to your child about what is on the screen. Communication is essential to the parent-child dyad.
- Provide your children with traditional toys and eliminate BST when engaging in play.
- Establish "screen-free zones" in your home.

References

Achtman, R., Green, C., & Bavelier, D. (2008). Video games as a tool to train visual skills. *Restorative Neurology and Neuroscience, 26*, 435-446.

American Academy of Pediatrics. (2013). Managing media: We need a plan. *AAP.org*. Retrieved from http://www.aap.org/en-us/about-the-aap/aap-press-room/pages/managing-media-we-need-a-plan.aspx

American Academy of Pediatrics, Committee on Public Education. (1999). Media education. *Pediatrics, 104*, 341-343.

American Academy of Pediatrics, Committee on Public Education. (2001). Children, adolescents, and television, policy statement. *Pediatrics, 107*(2), 423. doi:10.1542/peds.107.2.423

American Academy of Pediatrics, Committee on Public Education. (2011). Media education. *Pediatrics, 128*(5), 1-6. doi:10.1542/peds.2011-1753

American Psychological Association. (2005). *Resolution on violence in video games and interactive media*. Retrieved from https://www.apa.org/about/policy/interactive-media.pdf

Anderson, C. A., Gentile, D. A., & Buckley, K. E. (2007). *Violent video game effects on children and adolescents: Theory, research, and public policy*. New York, NY: Oxford University Press.

Anderson, C. A., Shibuya, A., Ihori, N., Swing, E., Bushman, B., Sakamoto, A., Rothstein, H., & Saleem, M. (2010). Violent video game effects on aggression, empathy, and prosocial behavior in eastern and western countries: A meta-analytic review. *Psychological Bulletin, 136*, 151-173.

Anderson, D. A., & Pempek, T. A. (2005). Television and very young children. *American Behavioral Scientist, 48*(5), 505-522.

Anderson, D. R., Bryant, J., Wilder, A., Santomero, A., Williams, M., & Crawley, A. M. (2000). Researching *Blue's Clues*: Viewing behavior and impact. *Media Psychology, 2*(2), 179-194.

Anderson, D. R., & Evans, M. K. (2001). Peril and potential of media for infants and toddlers. *Zero to Three, 22*(2), 10-16.

Anderson, D. R., Huston, A. C., Schmitt, K. L., Linebarger, D. L., & Wright, J. C. (2001). Early childhood television viewing and adolescent behavior: The recontact study. *Monographs of the Society for Research in Child Development, 66*(1), 1-147.

Armstrong, G., Bolarsky, G., & Mares, M. L.(1991). Background television and reading performance. *Communication Monographs, 58*(3), 235-253.

Armstrong, G. B., & Greenberg, B. S. (1990). Background television as an inhibitor of cognitive processing. *Human Communication Research, 16*, 355-386.

Bakeman, R., & Adamson, L. (1984). Coordinating attention to people and objects in mother-infant and peer-infant interaction. *Child Development, 55*, 1278-1289.

Baker, P., Keck, C. K., Mott, F. L., & Quinlan, S. V. (1993) NLSY Child Handbook: A Guide to the 1986-1990 National Longitudinal Survey of Youth Child Data. Revised Edition. Columbus, OH: Center for Human Resource Research, Ohio State University.

Bandura, A. (1963). The role of imitation in personality. *The Journal of Nursery Education, 18*(3), 591-601.

Bandura, A. (1965). Influence of models' reinforcement contingencies on the acquisition of imitative responses. *Journal of Personality and Social Psychology, 1*(6), 589-595.

Bandura, A., Ross, D., & Ross, S. A. (1963). Imitation of film-mediated aggressive models. *Journal of Abnormal and Social Psychology, 66*(1), 3-11.

Barr, R., & Hayne, H. (1999). Developmental changes in imitation from television during infancy. *Child Development, 70*(5), 1067-1081.

Bartholow, B. D., Sestir, M. A., & Davis, E. (2005). Correlates and consequences of exposure to video game violence: Hostile personality, empathy, and aggressive behavior. *Psychological Bulletin, 31*, 1573-1586.

Bates, J. E., Maslin, C. A., & Frankel, K. A. (1985). Attachment security, mother-child interaction, and temperament as predictors of behavior-problem ratings at age three years. *Society for Child Development Monographs, 209*, 167-193.

Bergen, D. (2007). Communicative actions and language narratives in preschoolers play with "talking" and "non-talking" action figures. In O. Jarrett & D. Sluss (Eds.), Play investigations in the 21st century (Play and Culture Series, Vol. 7, J. Johnson, Series Ed., pp. 229-248). Lanham, MD: University Press of America.

Berk, L. E. (2010, February). *Make-believe play: Wellspring for development of self-regulation.* Plenary presentation at UCB Interprofessional Continuing Education's The Early Years Conference: The Rights of the Child, Victoria, Canada.

Bjorklund, D. F., Yunger, J., & Pellegrini, A. D. (2002). The evolution of parenting and evolutionary approaches to childrearing. In M. H. Bornstein (Ed.), *Handbook of parenting: Practical issues in parenting* (2nd Edition, Vol. 5, pp. 3-30). Mahwah, NJ: Lawrence Erlbaum Associates.

Bornstein, M. H. (Ed.). (2002). *Handbook of parenting: Biology and ecology of parenting.* (2nd ed., Vol. 2). Mahwah, NJ: Lawrence Erlbaum Associates.

Brown v. Entertainment Merchants Association, 564 U.S. (2011).

Bruner, J. S. (1975). The ontogenesis of speech acts. *Journal of Child Language, 2*, 1-19.

Buckleitner, W. (2008). The state of children's interactive media. *Exchange, 179*, 62-65. Retrieved from http://www.ChildCareExchange.com

Burton, S. G., Calonico, J. M., & McSeveny, D. R. (1979). Effects of preschool television watching on first-grade children. *Journal of Communication, 29*(3), 164-170.

Bushman, B. J., & Anderson, C. A. (2009). Comfortably numb: Desensitizing effects of violent media on helping others. *Psychological Science, 20*, 273-277.

Business Wire. (2007). The worldwide market for edutainment toys is predicted to reach $7.3 billion by 2011. Retrieved August 2014 http://www.businesswire.com/news/home/20070502005509/en/Worldwide-Market-Edutainment-Toys-Predicted-Reach-7.3

Calvert, S. L., Rideout, V. J., Woolard, J. L., Barr, R. F., & Strouse, G. A. (2005). Age, ethnicity, and socioeconomic patterns in early computer use. *American Behavioral Scientist, 48*(5), 590-607. doi:10.1177/0002764204271508

Carnagey, N. L., Anderson, C. A., & Bushman, B. J. (2007). The effect of video game violence on physiological desensitization to real-life violence. *Journal of Experimental and Social Psychology, 43*, 489-496.

Christakis, D. A. (2011). The effects of fast-paced cartoons. *Pediatrics, 128*(4). 1-3. doi:10.1542/peds2011-2071

Christakis D. A., Gilkerson, J., Richards J. A., Garrison, M. M., Xu, D., Gray, S., & Yapanel, U. (2009). Audible TV is associated with decreased adult words, infant vocalization, and conversational turns: A population based study. Archives of *Pediatrics & Adolescent Medicine, 163*(6), 554-558.

Christakis, D. A., Zimmerman, F. J., DiGiuseppe, D. L., & McCarty, C. A. (2004). Early television exposure and subsequent attentional problems in children. *Pediatrics, 113*(4), 708-713.

Corapci, F., & Wachs, T. D. (2000). Does parental mood or efficacy mediate the influence of environmental chaos upon parenting behavior? *Merrill-Palmer Quarterly, 48*, 182-201.

Council on Communications and Media. (2011). Media use by children younger than 2 years. *Pediatrics, 128*(5), 1040-1045. doi:10.1542/peds.2011-1753

Critics zap video games: Senators urge government action to curb video-game violence. (1994). Referenced in Prot, S., McDonald, K., Anderson, C., & Gentile, D. (2012). Video games: Good, bad, or other? *Pediatric Clinics of North America, 59*(3), 647-658..

Davidson, J. L. F. (1998). Language and play: Natural partners. In E. P. Fromberg & D. Bergen (Eds.), *Play from birth to twelve and beyond: Contexts, perspectives, and meaning* (pp. 175-183). New York, NY: Garland.

DeGaetano, G. (2004). *Parenting well in a media age.* Fawnskin, CA: Personhood Press.

De Lacey, M. (2012, June 19). Mothers now prefer handing over smartphones rather than dummies to comfort crying babies. *Daily Mail Online.* Retrieved from http:// www.dailymail.co.uk/ femail/article-2161533/Mothers-prefer-smartphones-dummies-comfort-crying-babies.html

Dorr, A., Rabin, B., & Irlen, S. (2002). Parenting in a multimedia society. In M. H. Bornstein (Ed.), *Handbook of parenting: Practical issues in parenting* (2nd Edition, Vol. 5, pp. 349-374). Mahwah, NJ: Lawrence Erlbaum Associates.

Dworkin, M. (Ed.). (1970). *The literature of cinema.* New York, NY: Arno Press and the New York Times.

Elias, C., & Berk, L. E. (2002). Self-regulation in young children: Is there a role for sociodramatic play? *Early Childhood Research Quarterly, 17*(2), 216-238. doi:10.1016/S0885-2006(02)00146-1

Entertainment Software Association. (2013). Essential facts about the computer and video game industry. Retrieved from: http://www.isfe.eu/sites/isfe.eu/files/attachments/esa_ef_2013.pdf

Evans, M. K. (2003). *The effects of background television on very young children's play with toys* (Unpublished doctoral dissertation). University of Massachusetts, Amherst.

Fagot, B. I., Gauvain, M. D., & Kavanagh, K. (1996). Infant attachment and mother-child problem solving: A replication. *Journal of Social and Personal Relationships, 13,* 295-302.

Federal Bureau of Investigation. (2009). *Crime in the United States.* Retrieved from http://www2.fbi.gov/ucr/cius2008/

Ferguson, C., Rueda, S., Cruz, A., Ferguson, D., & Fritz, S. (2008). Violent video games and aggression: Causal relationship or byproduct of family violence and intrinsic violence motivation? *Criminal Justice and Behavior, 35*(3), 311-332.

Flavell, J. H., & Flavell, E. R. (1990). Do young children think of television images as pictures or real objects? *Journal of Broadcasting & Electronic Media, 34*(4), 399-480.

Funk, J., Brouwer, J., Curtiss, K., & McBroom, E. (2009). Parents of preschoolers: Expert media recommendations and ratings knowledge, media-effects beliefs, and monitoring practices. *Pediatrics, 123*(3), 981-988.

Gadberry, S. (1980). Effects of restricting first graders' television viewing on leisure time use, IQ change and cognitive style. *Journal of Applied Developmental Psychology, 1*(1), 45-58.

Garrison, M. M., & Christakis, D. A. (2005). *A teacher in the living room? Educational media for babies, toddlers, and preschoolers* (Issue Brief No. 7427). Menlo Park, CA: Henry J. Kaiser Family Foundation.

Gentile, D. (2009). Pathological video-game use among youth ages 8 to 18: A national study. *Psychological Science, 20*, 594-602.

Gentile, D., Walsh, D. (2002). A normative study of family media habits. *Applied Developmental Psychology, 23*, 157-178. Gottfried, A. W. (Ed.). (1984). Home environment and early cognitive development: Longitudinal research. Orlando, FL: Academic Press.

Gottfried, A.W. (1984). *Home Environment and Early Cognitive Development: Longitudinal Research.* Orlando, FL: Academic Press.

Greitemeyer, T., Osswald, S. (2010). Effects of prosocial video games on prosocial behavior. *Journal of Personality and Social Psychology, 98*(2), 211-221.

Groer, M., & Howell, M. (1990). Autonomic and cardiovascular responses of preschool children to television programs. *Journal of Child and Adolescent Psychiatric and Mental Health Nursing, 3*(4), 134-138.

Grusec, J. E., & Goodnow, J. J. (1994). Impact of parental discipline methods on the child's internalization of values: A reconceptualization of current points of view. *Developmental Psychology, 30*, 4-19.

Guernsey, L. (2007). *Into the minds of babes.* New York, NY: Basic Books.

Hart, B., & Risley, T. R. (1995) *Meaningful differences in the everyday experiences of young American children.* Baltimore, MD: Paul H. Brookes.

Hoff, E., & Naigles, L. (2002). How children use input to acquire a lexicon. *Child Development, 73*, 418-433.

Huston, A., & Bentley, A. (2010). Human development in societal context. *Annual Review of Psychology, 61*(1), 411-437, C1.

Huston-Stein, A., Fox, S., Greer, D., Watkins, B. A., & Whitaker, J. (1981). The effects of TV action and violence on children's social behavior. *Journal of Genetic Psychology, 138*(2), 183-191.

Jago, R., Stamatakis, E., Gama, A., Carvalhal, I., Nogueira, H., Rosado, V., & Padez, C. (2012). Parent and child screen-viewing time and home media environment. *American Journal of Preventive Medicine, 43*(2), 150-158. doi:10.1016/j.amepre.2012.04.012

Johnson, J., Brook, J., Cohen, P., & Kasen, S. (2007). Extensive television viewing and the development of attention and learning difficulties during adolescence. *Archives of Pediatrics & Adolescent Medicine, 161*(5), 480-486.

Jowett, G., Jarvie, K., & Fuller, K. (1996). *Children and the movies: Media influence and the Payne Fund controversy.* New York, NY: Cambridge University Press.

Kaiser Family Foundation (2005). The Effects of Electronic Media on Children Ages Zero to Six: A History of Research. Prepared for the Kaiser Family Foundation by the Center on Media and Child Health, Children's Hospital Boston.

Kirkorian, H. L. (2004). *The influence of background television on parent-child interaction* (Unpublished master's thesis). University of Massachusetts, Amherst.

Kirkorian H. L., Pempek, T. A., Murphy L. A., Schmidt, M. E., & Anderson, D. R. (2009). The impact of background television on parent-child interaction. *Child Development, 80*(5), 1350-1359.

Knowledge@Wharton (Producer). (2007, July 25). *Robbing the cradle? If marketers get their way, that bundle of joy can cost a bundle* [Audio podcast and transcript]. Retrieved from http://knowledge.wharton.upenn.edu/article/robbing-the-cradle-if-marketers-get-their-way-that-bundle-of-joy-can-cost-a-bundle/

Kochanska, G. (1995). Children's temperament, mothers' discipline, and security of attachment: Multiple pathways to emerging internalization. *Child Development, 66,* 597-615.

Kopp, C. B. (1982). Antecedents of self-regulation: A developmental perspective. *Developmental Psychology, 18*(2), 199-214. doi:10.1037/0012-1649.18.2.199

Landhuis, E. C., Poulton, R., Welch, D., & Hancox, R. J. (2008). Programming obesity and poor fitness: The long-term impact of childhood television. *Obesity, 16*(6), 1457-1459.

Lapierre, M. A., Piotrowski, J. T., & Linebarger, D. L. (2012). Background television in the homes of US children. *Pediatrics, 130*(5), 1-8. doi:10.1542/peds.2011-2581

Lavigne, H. J., Hanson, K. G., Pempeck, T. A., Kirkorian, H. L., & Anderson, D. R. (2011, April). *Baby video viewing and quantity and quality of parent language.* Poster presented at the biennial meeting of the Society for Research in Child Development, Montreal, Canada.

Lee, S. J., Bartolic, S., Vandewater, E. A. (2009). Predicting children's media use in the USA: Differences in cross-sectional and longitudinal analysis. *British Journal of Developmental Psychology, 27*(1), 123-143.

Lenhart, A., Kahne, J., Middaugh, E., Macgill, A., Evans, C., & Vitak, J. (2008). *Teens, video games and civics*. Retrieved from Pew Research Center website: http://www.pewinternet.org/files/old-media/Files/Reports/2008/PIP_Teens_Games_and_Civics_Report_FINAL.pdf.pdf

Lillard, A. S., & Peterson, J. (2011). The immediate impact of different types of television on young children's executive function. *Pediatrics, 128*(4), 644-649.

Linebarger, D. L., & Walker, D. (2005). Infants' and toddlers' television viewing and language outcomes. *American Behavioral Scientist, 48*(5), 624-645.

Lorch, E. P., Anderson, D. R., & Levin, S. R. (1979). The relationship of visual attention to children's comprehension of television. *Child Development, 50*(3), 722-727.

Lorch, E. P., & Castle, V. J. (1997). Preschool children's attention to television: Visual attention and probe response times. *Journal of Experimental Child Psychology, 66*(1), 111-127.

Lovaas, O. I. (1961). Effect of exposure to symbolic aggression on aggressive behavior. *Child Development, 32*, 37-44.

Luckin, R., Connolly, D., Plowman, L., & Airey, S. (2003). Children's interactions with interactive toy technology. *Journal of Computer Assisted Learning, 19*, 2, 165-176.

Luke, C. (1990). *Constructing the child viewer: A history of the American discourse on television and children, 1950–1980*. New York, NY: Praeger.

Maccoby, E. E. (1954). Why do children watch television? *Public Opinion Quarterly, 18*, 239-244.

Manganello, J. A., & Taylor, C. A. (2009). Television exposure as a risk factor for aggressive behavior among 3-year-old children. *Archives of Pediatrics & Adolescent Medicine, 163*(11), 1037-1045.

Masur, E. F., & Flynn, V. (2008). Infant and mother-infant play and the presence of the television. *Journal of Applied Developmental Psychology, 29*, 76-83.

Mayo Clinic. (2013, August 16). Children and TV: Limiting your child's screen time. *mayoclinic.org*. Retrieved from http://www.mayoclinic.org/healthy-lifestyle/childrens-health/in-depth/children-and-tv/art-20047952

McArthur, D., & Adamson, L. B. (1996). Joint attention in preverbal children: Autism and developmental language disorder. *Journal of Autism and Developmental Disorders, 26*, 481-496.

McCune, L. (1992). First words: A dynamic systems view. In C. A. Ferguson, L. Menn, & C. Stoel-Gammon (Eds.), *Phonological development: Models, research, implications* (pp. 313-335). Timonium, MD: York.

Mendelsohn, A., Brockmeyer, C., Dreyer, B. P., Fierman, A. H., Berkule-Silbermann, S., & Tomopoulous, S. (2010). Do verbal interactions with infants during electronic media exposure mitigate adverse impacts on their language development as toddlers? *Infant and Child Development, 19*, 577-593.

Mistry, K. B., Minkovitz, C. S., Strobino, D. M., & Borzekowski, D. L. (2007). Children's television exposure and social outcomes at 5.5 years: Does timing of exposure matter? *Pediatrics, 120*(4), 762-769.

Mumme, D. L., & Fernald, A. (2003). The infant as onlooker: Learning from emotional reactions observed in a television scenario. *Child Development, 74*(1), 221-237.

Murphy, R., Penuel, W., Means, B., Korbak, C., Whaley, A. (2002). E-DESK: *A review of recent evidence on the effectiveness of discrete educational software* (SRI Project 11063). Menlo Park, CA: SRI International.

Murray, F. (1972). The acquisition of conversation through social interaction. *Developmental Psychology, 6*, 1-6.

National Institute of Child Health and Human Development (NICHD), Early Child Care Research Network. (2003). Do children's attention processes mediate the link between family predictors and school readiness? *Developmental Psychology, 39*, 581-593.

National Scientific Council on the Developing Child. (2011). *Inbrief: The impact of early adversity on children's development*. Retrieved from http://developingchild.harvard.edu/wp-content/uploads/2015/05/inbrief-adversity-1.pdf

Nielson Report (2013). *The mobile consumer: A global snapshot*. Retrieved from http://www.nielsen.com/content/dam/corporate/us/en/reports-downloads/2013%20Reports/Mobile-Consumer-Report-2013.pdf

Pagani, L., Fitzpatrick, C., Barnett, T. A., & Dubow, E. (2010). Prospective associations between early childhood television exposure and academic, psychosocial, and physical well-being by middle childhood. *Archives of Pediatrics & Adolescent Medicine, 164*(5), 425-431.

Page, A. S., Cooper, A. R., Griew, P., & Jago, R. (2010). Children's screen viewing is related to psychological difficulties irrespective of physical activity. *Pediatrics, 126*(5), 1011-1017.

Pastor, D. L. (1981). The quality of mother-infant attachment and its relationship to toddlers' initial sociability with peers. *Developmental Psychology, 17*, 326-225.

Pearl, D., Bouthilet, L., & Lazar, J. B. (1982). *Television and behavior: Ten years of scientific progress and implications for the eighties*. Rockville, MD: U.S. Dept. of Health and Human Services.

Pempek, T. A., Kirkorian, H. L., & Anderson, D. R. (2010, March). *The impact of background TV on the quantity and quality of parents' verbal input.* Paper presented at the biannual International Conference on Infant Studies, Baltimore, MD.

Piaget, J. (1932). *Play, dreams, and imitation.* New York, NY: W. W. Norton & Company.

Prot, S., McDonald, K., Anderson, C., & Gentile, D. (2012). Video games: Good, bad, or other? *Pediatric Clinics of North America, 59*(3), 647-658.

Resnick, M. (2006). Computer as paintbrush: Technology, play, and the creative society. In D. G. Singer, R. M. Golinkoff, & K. Hirsch-Pasek (Eds.), *Play = Learning* (pp. 192-206). New York, NY: Oxford University Press.

Rhodes, R., Warburton, D., & Bredin, S. S. (2009). Predicting the effect of interactive video bikes on exercise adherence: An efficacy trial. Psychology, *Health & Medicine, 14,* 631-640.

Rice, M. L., Huston, A. C., Truglio, R., & Wright, J. C. (1990). Words from "Sesame Street": Learning vocabulary while viewing. *Developmental Psychology, 26*(3), 421-428.

Rich, M. (2007). Is television healthy? The medical perspective. In N. Pecora, J. P. Murray, & E. A. Wartella (Eds.), *Children and television: Fifty years of research* (pp. 109-147). Mahwah, NJ: Lawrence Erlbaum Associates.

Rideout, V. (2013). *Zero to eight: Children's media use in America.* San Francisco, CA: Commonsense Media.

Rideout, V. Foehr, U., & Roberts, D. (2010). *Generation m² media in the lives of 8 to 18 year olds* (Report No. 8010). Menlo Park, CA: Henry J. Kaiser Family Foundation.

Rideout, V., & Hamel, E. (2006, May). *The media family: Electronic media in the lives of infants,* toddlers, preschoolers, and their parents (Report No. 7500). Menlo Park, CA: Henry J. Kaiser Family Foundation.

Rideout, V., Vandewater, E., & Wartella, E. (2003, Fall). *Zero to six: Electronic media in the lives of infants, toddlers, and preschoolers* (Report No. 3378). Menlo Park, CA: Henry J. Kaiser Family Foundation.

Ritchel, M., & Stone, B. (2007, November 29). For toddlers, toy of choice is a tech device. *The New York Times.* Retrieved from www.nytimes.com/2007/11/29/technology/29techtoys.html

Roberts, D., Foehr, U. (2004). *Kids and media in America.* United Kingdom: Cambridge University Press.

Roberts, D., Foehr, U., Rideout, V., and Brodie, M. (1999). *Kids & media @ the new millennium: A comprehensive national analysis of children's media use.* Menlo Park, CA: Henry J. Kaiser Family Foundation. Retrieved from https://kaiserfamilyfoundation.files. wordpress.com 2013/01/kids-media-the-new-millennium-report.pdf

Roberts, D. F., Foehr, U. G., & Rideout, V. (2006). *Generation M: Media in the lives of 8–18 year-olds* (Report No. 7251). Menlo Park, CA: Henry J. Kaiser Family Foundation.

Rolandelli, D. R., Wright, J. C., Huston, A. C., & Eakins, D. (1991). Children's auditory and visual processing of narrated and non-narrated television programming. *Journal of Experimental Child Psychology, 51*(1), 90-122.

Russ, S. W. (2004). *Play in child development and psychotherapy.* Mahwah, NJ: Lawrence Erlbaum Associates.

Schmidt, M. E., Bickham, D. S., King, B. E., Slaby, R. G., Branner, A. C., & Rich, M. (2005). *The effects of electronic media on children ages zero to six: A history of research* (Issue Brief 7239). Menlo Park, CA: The Henry J. Kaiser Family Foundation.

Schmidt, M. E., Pempek, T. A., Kirkorian, H. L., Lund, A. F., & Anderson, D. R. (2008). The effects of background television on the toy play behavior of very young children. *Child Development, 79*(4), 1137-1151.

Schmidt, M. E., Rich, M., Rifas-Shiman, S. L., Oken, E., & Taveras, E. M. (2009). Television viewing in infancy and child cognition at 3 years of age in a US cohort. *Pediatrics, 123*(3), 370-375. doi:10.1542/peds.2008-3221

Sestir, M. A., & Bartholow, B. D. (2010). Violent and nonviolent video games produce opposing effects on aggressive and prosocial outcomes. *Journal of Experimental Social Psychology, 46*, 934-942.

Shimada, S., & Hiraki, K. (2006). Infant's brain responses to live and televised action. *Neuroimage, 32*(2), 930-939. doi:10.1016/j.neuroimage.2006.03.044

Sigman, A. (2007). Visual voodoo: The biological impact of watching television. *Biologist, 54*, 14-19.

Sigman, A. (2009). Well connected? The biological implications of 'social networking.' *Biologist, 56*, 14-20.

Sigler, J. (1997). *Education: Ends and means.* (Vol. 2). Lynchburg College Symposium Readings, University Press of America.

Silver, K. (2011). Best baby apps. *Parents Magazine.* Retrieved March 2, 2016, from http://www.parents.com/fun/entertainment/gadgets/best-iphone-apps-for-baby/

Singer, D. G., & Singer, J. L. (1980). Television viewing and aggressive behavior in preschool children: A field study. *Annals of the New York Academy of Sciences, 347*, 289-303.

Singer, D. G., Singer, J. L., Plaskon, S. L., & Schweder, A. E. (2003). Encouraging school readiness through guided pretend games. In S. Olfman (Ed.), *All work and no play: How educational reforms are harming our preschoolers* (pp. 59-101). Westport, CT: Greenwood.

Slade, A. (1987). A longitudinal study of maternal involvement and symbolic play during the toddler period. *Child Development, 58*, 367-375.

St. Peters, M., Fitch, M., Huston, A. C., Wright, J. C., & Eakins, D. J. (1991). Television and families: What do young children watch with their parents? *Child Development, 62*(6). 1409.

Swing, E. L., Gentile, D. A., Anderson, C. A., & Walsh, D. (2010). Television and video game exposure and the development of attention problems. *Pediatrics, 126*(2), 214-221.

Tamazashvili, T. (2007). Number of televisions in the US. In G.Elert (Ed.), *The Physics Factbook*. Retrieved from http://hypertextbook.com/facts/2007/TamaraTamazashvili.shtml

Taras, H. L., Sallis, J. F., Nader, P. R., & Nelson, J. (1990). Children's television-viewing habits and the family environment. *American Journal of Diseases of Children, 144*(3), 357-359.

Taylor, J. (2012). *Raising generation tech: Preparing your children for a media-fueled world*. Naperville, IL: Sourcebooks.

Thakkar, R. R., Garrison, M. M., & Christakis, D. A. (2006). A systematic review for the effects of television viewing by infants and preschoolers. *Pediatrics, 118*(5), 2025-2031.

Tinamura, M., Okuma, K., & Kyoshima, K. (2007). Television viewing, reduced parental utterances, and delayed speech development in infants and young children. *Archives of Pediatrics & Adolescent Medicine, 161*(6), 618-619.

Tomasello, M., & Farrar, M. J. (1986). Joint attention and early language. *Child Development, 57*, 1454-1463.

Tomopoulos, S., Brockmeyer Cates, C., Dreyer, B. P., Fierman, A. H., Berkule, S. B., & Mendelsohn, A. L. (2014). Children under the age of two are more likely to watch inappropriate background media than older children. *Acta Paediatrica, 103*(5), 546-552. doi:10.1111/apa.12588

Troseth, G. L., & DeLoache, J. S. (1998). The medium can obscure the message: Young children's understanding of video. *Child Development, 69*, 950-965. doi:19.1111/j.1467-8624.1998.tb06153.x

Vandewater, E. A., Bickham, D. S., Lee, J. H., Cummings, H. M., Wartella, E. A., & Rideout, V. J. (2006). When the television is always on: Heavy television exposure and young children's development. *American Behavioral Scientist, 48*(5), 562-577.

Vandewater, E. A., Park, S. E., Huang, X., & Wartella, E. A. (2005). No: You can't watch that—parental rules and young children's media use. *American Journal of Behavioral Science, 48*(5), 608-623.

Wall, B. (2006, November 24). Ambitious parents spend on educational toys for toddlers – Your Money - International Herald Tribune. *The New York Times*. Retrieved from www.nytimes.com/2006/11/24/your-money/24int-mtoys.3654661.html?pagewanted=1&_r=1

Wargo, J., Taylor, H. S., Alderman, N., Wargo, L., Bradley, J. M., & Addiss, S. (2012). *The cell phone problem*. Environment and Human Health Incorporated. Retrieved from: http://www.ehhi.org/reports/cellphones/cell_phone_report_EHHI_Feb2012.pdf

Wartella, E., & Reeves, R. (1985). Historical trends in research on children and the media: 1900–1960. *Journal of Communication, 35*(2), 118-133.

Watson, J. B. (1928). *Psychological care of infant and child*. New York, NY: W. W. Norton & Company.

Weber, D. S., & Singer, D. G. (2004). The media habits of infants and toddlers: Findings from a parent survey. *Zero to Three, 25*, 30-36.

Wong, W., Uribe-Zarain, X., Ma, W., Golinkoff, R. M., Fisher, K., & Hirsh-Pasek, K. (2008, March). "Educational toys": Do parents believe the hype? Poster presented at the XVI International Conference on Infant Studies, Vancouver, Canada.

Woodard, E. H., & Gridina, N. (2000). *Media in the home 2000: The fifth annual survey of parents and children* (Survey Series No. 7). Philadelphia: University of Pennsylvania. Retrieved from Annenberg Public Policy Center website: http://www.annenbergpublicpolicycenter.org/Downloads/Media_and_Developing_Child/mediasurvey/survey7.pdf

Wooldridge, M. B., (2010). *Playing with technology: Mother-toddler interaction and toys with batteries* (Master's thesis). Retrieved from UBC Open Library: https://circle.ubc.ca/bitstream/handle/2429/23711/ubc_2010_spring_wooldridge_michaela.pdf?sequence=1

Wright, J. C., Huston, A. C., Murphy, K. C., St Peters, M., Pinon, M., Scantlin, R., & Kotler, J. (2001). The relations of early television viewing to school readiness and vocabulary of children from low-income families: The early window project. *Child Development, 72*(5), 1347-1366.

Zigler, E. F., Singer, D. G., & Bishop-Josef, S. J., (Eds.). (2004). *Children's play: The roots of reading.* Washington, DC: Zero to Three.

Zimmerman, F. J., & Christakis, D. A., (2005). Children's television viewing and cognitive outcomes: A longitudinal analysis of national data. *Archives of Pediatrics & Adolescent Medicine, 159*(7), 619-625.

Zimmerman, F. J., Christakis, D. A., & Meltzoff, A. N. (2007). Television and DVD/video viewing in children younger than 2 years. *Archives of Pediatrics & Adolescent Medicine, 161*(5), 473-479.

Zimmerman, F. J., Gilkerson, J., Richards, J. A., Christakis, D. A., Xu, D., Gray, S., & Yapanel, U. (2009). Teaching by listening: The importance of adult/child conversations to language development. *Pediatrics, 124*(1), 342-349.

Structuring and Supporting Healthy Child Development: Parenting Practices in Relation to Feeding and Screen Time

Jessica Retan and Allison M. Hill

Abstract

There is increasing evidence of a strong relationship between parenting style and children's eating, screen time, and weight statuses. This paper reviews the literature on parenting style in relation to feeding practices, nutrition, and screen time. Feeding practices, as well as parenting styles, are categorized as authoritarian, authoritative, permissive–indulgent, and permissive–uninvolved. These styles are then associated with child health outcomes. The intersection of screen time in relation to parenting and the promotion of physical activity and healthy eating and sleeping habits is also discussed. Practical recommendations for parents and psychologists working with parents are offered using the Parent Development Theory (PDT).

Key words: parenting, parenting styles, nutrition, screen time, feeding practices, childhood obesity

Globally, the incidence of overweight children and childhood obesity among preschool-aged children increased from 4.2% in 1990 to 6.7% in 2010 (De Onis, Blossner, & Borghi, 2010). Concern over the matter is particularly acute in the United States, where an estimated 16.8% of children and adolescents under the age of 18 meet the criteria for obesity (Ogden, Carroll, Kit, & Flegal, 2012). Childhood obesity has been associated with a number of negative physical health problems, including increased risk of cardiovascular disease, diabetes, and many cancers (Daniels, 2006). Additionally, being overweight and obese in childhood is associated with significant reductions in quality of life (Williams, Wake, Hesketh, Maher,

& Waters, 2005) and a greater risk of experiencing bullying, social isolation, and teasing (Janssen, Craig, Boyce, & Pickett, 2004).

Increasingly, evidence links parenting practices with children's eating habits and weight status (Faith, Scanlon, Birch, Francis, & Sherry, 2004; Galloway, Fiorito, Francis, & Birch, 2006; Wardle & Carnell, 2007). Screen time, too, has been implicated in the child weight-problem equation (Mark & Janssen, 2008; Miller, Taveras, Rifas-Shiman, & Gillman, 2008). Parenting style has been identified as influential in the development of children's habits and preferences around eating and physical activity and thus contributes to children's weight status and health outcomes (Ventura & Birch, 2008). Of the many factors influencing childhood obesity—including the availability of healthful foods and the child's genetic predisposition—parenting style is unique in that it can be managed through education and behavioral interventions. Understanding the specific behaviors associated with effective and ineffective parenting is critical for the management of children's weight and the prevention of childhood obesity.

Parenting Styles and Feeding Practices

The literature on parenting styles has adhered closely to the classification system outlined by Baumrind (1971) and expanded upon by Maccoby and Martin (1983), which describes general parenting styles according to the dimensions of demandingness and responsiveness. *Demandingness* refers to the extent to which parents exert control, make maturity demands, and supervise their children's activities. *Responsiveness* refers to the extent to which parents show affective warmth, acceptance, and involvement with their children (Baumrind, 2005). Four general parenting styles emerge from this paradigm: authoritarian, authoritative, permissive–indulgent, and permissive–uninvolved. Parents who have an authoritarian style display high demandingness and low responsiveness; in general, their parenting is characterized by punitive, restrictive, and power-asserting behaviors. Parents who have an authoritative style are ranked high on both demandingness and responsiveness and generally show appropriate involvement with and nurturance of their children. Those who have a permissive–indulgent style display low demandingness and high responsiveness; their parenting is characterized by warmth, acceptance, and a lack of limit setting and monitoring. Finally, parents who are ranked low on both demandingness and responsiveness have a permissive–uninvolved or neglectful style, offering little nurturance, control, or involvement with their children (Maccoby & Martin).

General parenting style has been linked to the practice of *feeding*, which is used in the literature and in this paper to describe the feeding relationship, or, "the complex of interactions that takes places between parent and child as they engage in food selection, ingestion, and regulation behaviors" (Satter, 1986, p. 352). The feeding relationship is further described as the reciprocity that occurs when children send cues to their parents about their timing, amount, preference, pacing, and eating capabilities while parents, in turn, respond appropriately to these cues, eventually helping their children discriminate between these internal signals. An appropriate feeding relationship, according to Satter, can support children's achievement of developmental milestones and create positive regard for themselves and the world. The term *eating* will be used strictly to describe the behavior of ingesting food and beverages. Lastly, *nutrition* will be used in reference to the recommended daily amounts of fat, carbohydrates, protein, sugar, vitamins, and so forth that are ingested while eating.

Although general parenting style is distinct from specific child-feeding practices, research suggests considerable overlap between the two. A recent study using the Child Feeding Questionnaire (CFQ; Birch et al., 2001) and the Parenting Styles and Dimensions Questionnaire (PSDQ; Robinson, Mandleco, Olsen, & Hart, 2001) found that specific child-feeding practices that are identified in the nutrition literature as authoritarian, authoritative, and permissive predicted those same general parenting styles.

For example, the use of feeding practices such as restriction and pressure to eat—which are high on demandingness and low on responsiveness—predicted an overall authoritarian parenting style, and the use of feeding practices such as modeling and monitoring—which are high on both demandingness and responsiveness—predicted an overall authoritative parenting style (Hubbs-Tait, Kennedy, Page, Topham, & Harrist, 2008). For this reason, the nomenclature around parenting styles has been adapted to describe feeding practices, and the categories of authoritarian, authoritative, permissive–indulgent, and permissive–uninvolved provide a framework for discussing the literature on parenting and nutrition.

Authoritarian Feeding Practices

The majority of the research on feeding practices has focused on parents' efforts to control the food intake of their children through authoritarian feeding practices (Wardle & Carnell, 2007). Two such authoritarian practices—high on demandingness and low on responsiveness—are restriction and pressure to eat. Restriction involves limiting the availability of certain foods or children's access to those foods, and pressure to eat involves insisting that children eat more or different types of foods, forcing children to finish meals, or threatening to take something pleasurable away from children if they do not eat the desired food (Gevers, Kremers, de Vries, & van Assema, 2014). Parents using these practices may intend to promote healthier diets in their children, and perhaps even prevent obesity, but research suggests that such attempts can actually impede self-regulation by interfering with children's understanding of their own internal cues of hunger and satiety.

Generally, parental overcontrol of children's eating through restrictive practices tends to be associated with overeating and poor self-regulation of food intake in preschool-aged children (Faith et al., 2004). Restricting children's access to high-calorie foods may have the unintended effect of increasing rather than decreasing children's preferences for those foods (Benton, 2004). Additionally, imposing external controls on eating may impede children's ability to self-regulate their food intake, or it may promote eating in the absence of hunger, either of which could lead to excess weight gain. For example, Fisher and Birch (1999) investigated the effects of restricting children's access to palatable foods (apple or peach bar cookies) within their eating environment. Each child was observed on 10 occasions over a five-week period. During the restricted-access procedure, children had free access to a control food throughout a 20-minute period. In contrast, a restricted food was kept in a large transparent jar in the center of the table. After 10 minutes, children were allowed access to the restricted food for two minutes, followed by the removal of any uneaten portions of the restricted food. Results revealed that restricting access increased children's spontaneous response to the food. Although children initially indicated similar degrees of preference for the control and target foods, when restriction was imposed the restricted food elicited more positive comments and more requests, and when it was made available, children took larger portions and ate more compared to the freely accessible control food. These findings indicate that restricting access to palatable foods may be counterproductive in that it may promote their intake. Furthermore, longitudinal research reveals that, at least among middle-class, white families with daughters, maternal use of restrictive feeding practices predicts uninhibited overeating and greater weight gain (Birch, Fisher, & Davison, 2003).

Excessive pressure to eat may also influence children's overall dietary quality as well as their ability to regulate food intake and their preferences for healthy foods. Longitudinal research reveals that higher levels of parental control and pressure to eat are linked with lower fruit and vegetable consumption (Fisher, Mitchell, Smiciklas-Wright, & Birch, 2002) and higher consumption of dietary fat (Lee, Mitchell, Smiciklas-Wright, & Birch, 2001). Additionally, in a study of children's eating practices, encouraging children to eat by having them focus their attention on "cleaning their plate" promoted greater overall consumption and made children less sensitive to their own feelings of fullness (Birch, McPhee, Shoba, Steinberg, & Krehbiel, 1987). Moreover, pressure to eat has a negative effect on children's preferences for healthy foods. Galloway and colleagues found that when children were pressured to eat specific foods (e.g., "you must finish your soup"), children made more negative comments about the soup, consumed less of it, and had a decreased preference for the soup (Galloway et al., 2006). In addition to a causal effect of pressure on consumption and preference, Galloway and colleagues found that children with lower body mass index (BMI) scores were more likely to be pressured to eat at home and were less influenced by the experimentally manipulated pressure-to-eat session than their higher BMI peers. This finding suggests that parental use of pressure is triggered by concerns about the child's low weight status or low levels of food intake; however, pressuring children to eat does not have the desired effect on food preference or consumption. Other studies have found a decreased preference for healthy foods even when those foods are used as a contingency for a reward (Birch, Birch, Marlin, & Kramer, 1982; Birch, Marlin, & Rotter, 1984). Thus, pressuring children to eat vegetables in order to be allowed to leave the table or as a contingency to receiving dessert may ultimately lead to children disliking those vegetables.

Authoritative Feeding Practices

Authoritative feeding practices are also characterized by high demandingness or expectations placed on children when eating. Unlike authoritarian parents, however, those with authoritative styles also tend to be highly responsive to children's eating cues and behaviors. Responsive feeding involves attending to children's signals of hunger and satiety and reacting to children in a prompt, emotionally supportive, contingent, and developmentally appropriate way (Black & Aboud, 2011). In practice, these efforts may entail pacing feeding according to children's signals, providing gentle prompts to eat, but withdrawing those prompts if children refuse, and suggesting that children try new foods without coercion. By contrast, feeding that is not responsive may involve continuing with feeding even though children show signs of refusal, forcing food into their mouths, threatening or withholding preferred foods, and not being sensitive to the children's preferences. Responsive feeding has been linked to the development of positive eating habits in children. These habits include increased attentiveness and interest in eating, attunement to internal signals of hunger and satiety, ability to communicate needs to their caregiver with distinct and meaningful signals, and successful progression to independent feeding (Black & Aboud, 2011). These associations suggest that parents who feed responsively nurture children who are similarly responsive to their own internal cues, matching dietary intake closely with physiological need.

In addition to responsiveness, authoritative feeding practices include (a) modeling, such as eating healthy foods with the child and in the presence of the child; (b) appropriate monitoring by keeping track of the number and types of foods that the child eats; (c) providing rationales; (d) providing appropriate rules and structure by articulating expectations about when and where it is appropriate to eat, such as whether the child is allowed a snack shortly before a meal; (e) encouraging the child to try a large variety of foods; and (f) involving children, which includes allowing them to participate in selecting and preparing healthy foods (Hubbs-Tait et al., 2008; Hughes, Power, Fisher, Mueller, & Nicklas, 2005). These authoritative practices allow children some degree of autonomy and control over their own eating while structuring and supporting healthy choices.

Authoritative feeding practices are not likely used in isolation, but rather lend themselves to simultaneous use in terms of snacking, selecting food, and encouraging children to try new foods. For example, parents who are articulating a rule about snacking may want to accompany it with a health rationale, and parents who are involving their children in food selection and preparation can use the opportunity to educate and to encourage children to try new foods. Research supports the notion that authoritative feeding practices tend to accompany and reinforce each other. For example, in a structured play session with low-income, Mexican American families, children's knowledge and awareness of the relationship between nutrition and health was assessed in relation to the socialization strategies used by their mothers. After controlling for child age, mothers' provision of opportunities for children to participate in their own food decisions was positively associated with children's knowledge and awareness of the health consequences of eating habits, whereas the use of commands was negatively related (Hays, Power, & Olvera, 2001). These findings suggest that parents who engage their children in their own eating decisions through reasoning and explanation—and who use minimal external pressure to elicit child compliance—also foster their children's understanding of food choices and how those choices influence their health.

Whereas authoritative feeding practices have been linked to increased child self-regulation and nutritional knowledge, the authoritative parenting style in general has been associated with greater home availability of fruits and vegetables as well as greater child consumption of dairy, fruits, and vegetables and lower consumption of junk foods than that of authoritarian feeding practices (Patrick, Nicklas, Hughes, & Morales, 2005). Findings from the National Institute of Child Health and Human Development's *Study of Early Child Care and Youth Development* reveal a protective association of authoritative parenting style with risk of overweight status among 5-year-old children (NICHD Early Child Care Research Network, 2005). Among a national sample of socio-economically and ethnically diverse families with young children, authoritarian parents were nearly five times as likely to have an overweight child as authoritative parents, after adjusting for the potentially confounding effects of income and race (Rhee, Lumeng, Appugliese, Kaciroti,

& Bradley, 2006). These findings suggest that the consistent use of authoritative feeding practices, which set clear expectations for children's eating behavior and are responsive to children's needs, may reduce the risk of obesity.

Permissive Feeding Practices

Finally, feeding practices characterized by low demandingness or expectations placed on children while eating are considered permissive. Within the permissive style, parents may be more or less responsive to their children. Feeding practices that are low on demandingness and high on responsiveness are considered permissive–indulgent, whereas those that are low on both demandingness and responsiveness are permissive–uninvolved or neglectful (Birch et al., 2001; Robinson et al., 2001). In both cases, parents comply with the preferences of their children without setting limits.

Permissive feeding practices would logically appear to promote overeating among those children who are exposed to a dietary environment of abundance. Indeed, research suggests a strong association between permissive–indulgent feeding and weight status among low-income preschool children. Hughes and colleagues found that indulgent feeding practices were significantly correlated with child BMI after controlling for variables known to be associated with child BMI (e.g., ethnicity, child gender, parent BMI), demographics (e.g., parent education, parent age, child age), and psychosocial characteristics (e.g., parent affect and child temperament) (Hughes, Shewchuk, Baskin, Nicklas, & Qu, 2008). In a separate study of low-income African American and Hispanic families, children of parents using permissive–indulgent feeding practices had higher weight-status scores compared to children of authoritarian parents (Hughes et al., 2005). While permissive–indulgent feeding practices are predictive of higher child weight status, this assertion remains unproven with regard to permissive–uninvolved practices. In one study, neglected children, possibly reflecting the permissive–uninvolved parenting style, had a greater risk of adult obesity (Lissau & Sorensen, 1994). However, feeding styles and their effects on dietary intake were not considered. A separate study of dietary intake among low-income preschool children found that consumption of fruits and vegetables was lowest in children of permissive—both indulgent and uninvolved—parents compared to children of authoritarian and authoritative parents (Hoerr et al., 2009). These findings suggest that uninvolved parenting might result in poor diet quality in children, but not necessarily in overeating and in becoming overweight.

Demographic Trends

The demographic trends associated with different parenting styles and feeding practices have received limited attention in the literature, despite the fact that childhood obesity is disproportionately high among racial/ethnic minority children (Ogden et al., 2012). Many studies involving parenting styles and feeding practices have been conducted, for the most part, with middle-class, white samples (Faith et al., 2004; Ventura & Birch, 2008), though recent studies have sought to reverse this trend. For example, the Caregiver's Feeding Style Questionnaire (CFSQ) was developed specifically for use with low-income Hispanic and African American families; findings suggest a significant disparity in the feeding practices between these groups, with Hispanic parents engaging in more permissive–indulgent feeding and African American parents engaging in more permissive–uninvolved feeding (Hughes et al., 2005). Though differences across measures—for example, CFQ (Birch et al., 2001), Feeding Demands Questionnaire (FDQ; Faith, Storey, Kral, & Pietrobelli, 2008), and Food Parenting Practice Categories (FPPC; O'Connor et al., 2010)—render comparisons to a wider population problematic, the data collected by Hughes and colleagues (2005) provides an estimate of the proportion of low-income caregivers in the United States using each of the four feeding styles: 36.4% authoritarian, 14.7% authoritative, 34.6% permissive–indulgent, and 14.3% permissive–uninvolved. More specifically, authoritarian and permissive–indulgent feeding styles, which have the greatest relative odds of children becoming overweight (Rhee et al., 2006), were the most commonly used among caregivers in this low-income sample. Greater attention to and promotion of authoritative feeding practices is needed in order to reduce the prevalence of childhood obesity.

Nutrition and Screen Time

Another major influence on children's nutritional and physical health with regard to parenting is the presence of screen time, which is described as one's exposure to computers, handheld digital devices, movies, smartphones, television, and other visual devices (Mayo Clinic, 2013). The amount of screen time to which children are exposed and the content of the material, specifically in food and beverage commercials, can have an effect on children's nutritional intake and physical activity levels (Mark & Janssen, 2008; Wiecha et al., 2006). Current recommendations of children's health include limiting entertainment (non-educational) screen time to less than two hours per day (American Academy of Pediatrics, [AAP], 2013), engaging in moderate to vigorous physical activity for at least 60 minutes daily (Council on Sports Medicine and Fitness and Council on School Health, 2006), and sleeping 10-11 hours per night for children ages 6-10, and 8.5-9.5 hours for children ages 11-17 (National Sleep Foundation, 2014). In a recent study of children ages 7-12, children who followed each of these guidelines were significantly less likely to be overweight (i.e., 16% of boys and 9% of girls) compared to children who followed none of the guidelines (i.e., 53% of boys and 42.5% of girls), and each additional recommendation that was unmet increased children's chances of obesity in a graded manner (Laurson, Lee, Gentile, Walsh, & Eisenmann, 2014).

In addition to obesity, increased screen time has been shown to have a number of negative health consequences on children, including the risk of metabolic syndrome—a cluster of symptoms that includes increased blood pressure, high blood sugar levels, excess body fat around the waist, and abnormal cholesterol levels (Mark & Janssen, 2008). In children as young as 3 years old, each one-hour increment of television viewing is associated with increased consumption of fast food, processed meat, sugar-sweetened beverages, and trans fats in addition to lower intakes of calcium, dietary fiber, fruits, and vegetables (Miller et al., 2008). Furthermore, childhood obesity significantly increases the risk of adult obesity (Whitaker, Wright, Pepe, Seidel, & Dietz, 1997). For these reasons, the long-term implications of increased screen time merit discussion. Three implications in particular—decreased physical activity, the impact of food and drink advertisements, and disturbances in children's sleep patterns—are also areas in which parents can take meaningful steps to avert the negative consequences associated with screen time and help maintain their children's health.

Decreased Physical Activity

While, in general, authoritarian parents are more restrictive of their children's activities and permissive parents are less restrictive, research suggests that children's weight status is linked not simply to the presence of parental restriction, but rather to the *specific child behaviors* that are either permitted or restricted. Langer, Crain, Senso, Levy, and Sherwood (2014) examined the relationship between parenting style and physical activity with children who were either overweight or at risk for becoming overweight and discovered that both authoritarian and permissive parenting were associated with children's increased screen time use. However, permissive parents who supported children's physical activity (through encouraging, providing transportation, or watching children engage in physical activity or play sports) had more active children than authoritarian parents who also showed support for children's physical activity. Similar results were found in a study of parents whose children were given video games that required the children to be physically active to play. Here, parents who had more restrictive rules regarding television had children who were more sedentary and less physically active, whereas parents who were permissive about television rules, but *also* supported their children's physical activity had more active children (O'Connor, Chen, Baranowski, Thompson, & Baranowski, 2013).

From this research, it appears that permissive parents whose children may have more unstructured free time might increase physical activity by supporting children's efforts to spend their free time being active. Authoritarian parents may be more restrictive of screen time, but also more restrictive of physical activity (e.g., "no playing sports in the house"), which could increase sedentary time. Interestingly, authoritarian parents who restricted children's sedentary time by limiting screen time and requiring children to go outside after spending significant time indoors were found to have children who watched significantly less television than permissive parents (Malik, Pan, Willett, & Hu, 2013). With regard to reducing children's screen time, authoritarian parents who limit screen time and sedentary time (but not physical activity) are seemingly more successful than those who only limit screen time, and permissive parents who do not limit screen time are more successful if they also encourage children to spend their unstructured free time engaging in physical activity.

In light of these findings, certain children may be at especially high risk for the poor health outcomes associated with increased screen time. Tandon and colleagues (2012) found that children ages 6-11 from lower income households were more likely than their higher income peers to have a DVD player, a television, or video games in their bedrooms. Compared to their peers of higher socioeconomic status (SES), children in lower SES households had less access to portable play equipment such as bikes or jump ropes and more restrictive rules about using physical activity equipment (e.g., "do not ride your bike on the street"), which may be a reflection of parents' neighborhood safety concerns. In conjunction, these parenting practices in lower income households provided more opportunity for sedentary behavior. Parental restrictions on physical activity may put children at unique risk; previous research has shown that higher levels of vigorous exercise may be more influential in reducing the risk of childhood obesity than lower levels of sedentary time (Steele, van Sluijs, Cassidy, Griffin, & Ekelund, 2009). Overall, placing restrictions on or not supporting children's physical activity appears to be a more powerful predictor of poor health outcomes than solely placing limits on screen time.

Food and Beverage Advertisements

In addition to substituting physical activity with sedentary behavior, children with high screen time may also be affected by the advertisements that permeate television and online streaming websites such as YouTube. Recent research into the effects of middle-school children's viewing of commercials for candy, fast food, fried potatoes, salty snacks, sugar-sweetened beverages, and sweet baked snacks has shown that each additional hour of television viewing was associated with a 167-calorie increase in children's food consumption, specifically those foods that children had seen advertised on television (Wiecha et al., 2006). Another study of third-graders found that the more television children watched, the more they requested the food and drinks they saw advertised (Chamberlain, Wang, & Robinson, 2006).

However, a second phenomenon was found to occur with younger children aged 5-7, wherein researchers found that exposure to food advertisements resulted in increased total food intake post-viewing, not just requests for advertised foods (Halford, Boyland, Hughes, Oliveira, & Dovey, 2007). It may be that younger children are more likely to request brand-name processed food snacks after watching television *and* eat more overall after they have seen food advertisements. These findings suggest that even parents who do not abide by their children's requests for brand-name snacks may be putting their children at risk for increased BMI simply by allowing young children to be exposed to advertisements.

Buijzen, Schuurman, and Bomhof (2008) conducted a similar study of children aged 4-12 who viewed advertised food brands and found evidence of a "spill-over" effect of advertising in higher income children: Children who viewed more television ate more of the brands they saw on commercials and ate more high-calorie foods in the same product category. Notably, Buijzen and colleagues found that the relationship between television viewing and overall increased food consumption was significant only in lower income families.

In a follow-up study, Buijzen (2009) explored this phenomenon and found that parental communication moderated the effect of food advertising on children's overall food consumption. Specifically, Buijzen compared the effects of *active advertising mediation*, defined as "making deliberate comments and judgments about television commercials and explaining the nature and selling intent of advertising to children," versus *restrictive advertising mediation*, which included limiting or shielding children from advertising by reducing their exposure (Buijzen, 2009, pp.106-107). This study suggests that restrictive advertising mediation was effective for younger children ages 4-8, whereas active advertising mediation was effective for children of all ages in the study. In addition, children whose parents had strict and clear rules about what children could actually eat were also less likely to consume excess calories after watching advertisements. This study highlights the importance of age-appropriate strategies to reduce the effects of marketing on children's food requests; these strategies are also consistent with an authoritative parenting style. By combining high levels of control (e.g., restricting and/or appropriately monitoring young children's access to advertisements) with high levels of responsiveness (e.g., educating children about the nature of advertisements in order to foster their independent decision-making), these parents were most successful in reducing the effects of food advertisements on their children's intake of high-calorie foods.

With regard to advertisements, certain demographic groups were found to be at higher risk for the negative health outcomes associated with increased television watching. Outley and Taddese (2006) compared advertisements during after-school hours on Black Entertainment Television (BET), the Disney Channel, and The WB and found that BET had significantly more food and beverage advertisements. Specifically, 36.3% of BET's food and beverage advertisements were for fast food restaurants, 31.3% were for sugary drinks, 16.8% were for candy, 13.7% were for cereals, and 2.0% were for snacks. Health-related content and physical activity-related content were shown in less than 10% of the commercials across networks; however, researchers found that this content often was not connected directly to the product. Therefore, this health-related content may have been so subtle or implied that the message was not noticeable to the children viewers. Because BET is directly marketed to the African American community, these children may be at higher risk for overexposure to food and beverage advertisements that are negatively related to children's eating habits.

Disturbances in Sleep Patterns

The presence of television and other media devices in children's bedrooms also may impact children's health by reducing, delaying, or interfering with the quality of their sleep. Even when controlling for physical activity and frequency of television watching, those children with a television in their bedroom who watched at least one session per day were more likely to be overweight (Adachi-Mejia et al., 2006). In addition, research has shown that watching more than 1.5 hours of television per day made children ages 4-8 more likely to be overweight (de Jong et al., 2011) and also more likely to have shorter sleep duration (de Jong et al., 2012). Furthermore, the likelihood that children would watch more than 1.5 hours of television increased for children who had a television in their bedroom, more than two televisions in the house, or no rules on television watching. Interestingly, de Jong and colleagues

(2012) did not find lower levels of physical activity in the children who watched more than 1.5 hours per day, but they did find that children's shorter sleep duration was associated with eating candy without asking permission, going to bed late, spending less time with their caretakers, and watching television during meals.

These findings indicate that the behaviors of permissive or indulgent parents cross the domains of food and screen time, such that parents with low levels of control or involvement in their child's nutrition also allow ungoverned screen time consumption. The lack of regulation associated with a permissive parenting style may also cause biological hormonal changes in children's bodies. Research indicates that children and adults with shorter sleep duration have increased levels of the hormone leptin and decreased levels of ghrelin, which are responsible for appetite regulation (Van Cauter & Knutson, 2008). Therefore, in households with inconsistent or nonexistent rules about bedtime, food choices, and screen time, children who sleep less may have increased appetite and decreased regulation of food intake.

In addition to sleeping less, increased screen time has been associated with delayed sleep onset. For older children, the absence of an established bedtime and limits on screen time can result in dramatically increased calorie consumption. In obese adolescents, those who went to bed later than 3:30 a.m. had an increased daily intake of 425 calories in addition to increased screen time (Adamo, Wilson, Belanger, & Chaput, 2013). Yet, Adamo and colleagues' findings report no difference in sleep duration between "normal" and "late" sleepers. That is, while getting the same amount of sleep, adolescents who used more screen time also went to bed later and in turn ate 27% more calories than their earlier-bedtime counterparts.

Children who consumed caffeine also showed an increased risk of sleep disturbances. A study of 10- to 17-year-old Hispanic and Caucasian adolescents reported increased BMI to be associated with less sleep (Drescher, Goodwin, Silva, & Quan, 2011). Of those who slept less, older adolescents were more likely to drink caffeine, while younger adolescents were more likely to have more screen time. This research suggests that adolescents who get less sleep may have parents who set fewer rules about both screen time and caffeine consumption through coffee, energy drinks, or sodas. According to the research, the parental behaviors associated with these sleep disturbances (e.g., allowing children to have a television in the bedroom, not putting limits on television viewing, and not giving children regular bedtimes) are consistent with a permissive or indulgent parenting style. By not establishing rules for screen time, bedtimes, and food consumption at an early age, parents may not be able to impart the necessary self-regulatory strategies that children need to maintain healthy eating and sleep habits.

Parental Interventions

Different parenting styles are associated with the amount and quality of nutrition, physical activity, screen time, and sleep that children receive throughout their development. In considering parenting and how psychologists may assist individuals in their important child-rearing role, Mowder's (2005) Parent Development Theory (PDT) provides a useful framework. The PDT asserts that the role of parent is not exclusively biological, but associated with certain behaviors that define the parental role. In general, the parent role consists of the recognition, acceptance, and performance of the parent role. The parent-role characteristics associated with the parent role fall into six domains: *bonding*, *discipline*, *education*, *general welfare and protection*, *responsivity*, and *sensitivity*.

Briefly, *bonding* includes showing affection, warmth, and caring toward children and endeavoring to make children feel loved. *Discipline* involves providing and discussing rules and assuring that children are responsive to them. *Education* is primarily the transmission of information in order to inform and guide children. *General welfare and protection* includes protecting children from harm and ensuring that their basic needs are met, such as the need for food, water, and shelter. *Responsivity*, within PDT, refers to interacting with, listening to, and responding to children; and *sensitivity* refers to understanding children's needs and matching parental responses to perceived needs (Mowder, 2005).

The relative importance of each of these parent-role characteristics changes over time in response to children's changing developmental needs (Mowder, 2005). Moreover, the six parent-role characteristics are not mutually exclusive. That is, specific parenting behaviors may incorporate elements of multiple parent-role characteristics. As we consider recommendations for parents gleaned from the literature on child physical development, it is noteworthy that many of these "best practices" for parents constitute an integration of multiple parent-role characteristics. The parent-role characteristics of the PDT and the specific recommendations outlined below are presented here to facilitate discussions between psychologists and parents regarding children's healthy physical development.

Using the PDT to Communicate with Parents

Psychologists and health care providers have opportunities to help educate parents about the important role they play as children's "nutritional gatekeepers" who acquire and prepare the food for their families and establish routines around bedtimes, mealtimes, physical activity, and screen time (Wansink, 2002). The following is a summary of educational and behavioral interventions based on the PDT parent-role characteristics that psychologists can recommend to parents to promote children's healthy physical development.

Educate children about food commercials. Rather than trying to shield children from viewing food commercials, actively talking to children about the way commercials are designed to make them want the foods they see can limit children's cravings for these foods in children as young as 4 years of age (Buizjen, 2009).

Eat meals together, without television. For many families, eating meals together is a time for parents to bond with children.

Eating family dinners together has been correlated to increased fruit, vegetable, and key nutrient intake as well as decreased intake of soft drinks in adolescents (Larson, Neumark-Sztainer, Hannan, & Story, 2007). While eating meals together may be a bonding activity for families, the presence of the television may limit parents' ability to be responsive by reducing the interactions between them and their children. Recent research has shown that the odds that vegetables will be served at dinner decreases with each night that families eat dinner while watching television (FitzPatrick, Edmunds, & Dennison, 2007). It is likely that parents' ability to engage and respond appropriately to children during meal times may be hindered by the distraction of television.

Learn and employ strategies for talking to children about food. Parents who are informed about nutrition and advertising strategies are better able to talk to their children about healthy food choices. Hindman and Morrison (2011) found that parents from Head Start programs who enrolled in a media literacy education curriculum and were taught practical strategies—such as how to distinguish between truths and claims in advertising, how to read food labels, and how talk to their children about requesting advertised foods while grocery shopping—reported changes in their own behavior, attitudes, and knowledge about advertising and in their children's food requests. Parent education is especially important for low-income families whose children may be more susceptible to requesting advertised foods and consuming more calories after viewing food advertisements (Buizjen et al., 2008).

Provide healthy drink alternatives. One of the biggest contributors to increased BMI is children's consumption of sugar-sweetened beverages (Malik et al., 2013) Recent research has shown that children whose parents substituted water or milk for one sugar-sweetened beverage daily over a six-year period had significantly lower BMI than those children whose parents did not limit their sugar-sweetened beverage consumption (Zheng et al., 2014). This research suggests that parents who limit but do not entirely forbid sugar-sweetened beverages may be successful at helping children maintain a healthy weight over time.

Remove television from children's bedrooms. The presence of a television in the bedroom has been linked to higher incidences of children's obesity (Adachi-Mejia et al., 2006; Dennison, Erb, & Jenkins, 2002) and shorter sleeping times (de Jong et al., 2012). Interventions that include recommendations to remove televisions from the bedroom as part of a multi-faceted parental education program have been shown effective in reducing childhood obesity (Stahl, Necheles, Mayefsky, Wright, & Rankin, 2011; Taveras, 2011). In addition, a bedtime ritual that includes parents reading or singing to children has been shown to increase both sleep duration and children's verbal test scores (Hale, Berger, LeBourgeois, & Brooks-Gunn, 2011). Bedtime offers a special time for parents and children to bond, and by replacing television with reading or singing, parents may be able to help children improve their sleep habits.

Set rules about television and explain them to children. A survey of more than 7,000 participants ages 9 to 15 found that children were more likely to exceed the recommended daily limit of screen time (120 minutes) if their parents did not have or did not consistently enforce rules about screen time use. For those children who reported that their parents did have rules about the amount of television they could watch and video games they could play, children were less likely to exceed them if they agreed with their parents and if parents themselves were correctly informed about the recommended daily amount of screen time (Carlson et al., 2010).

Support physical activity in children. In regard to physical activity, there is evidence to suggest that parents are more likely to spend time with their children watching television or DVDs than engaging in physical activity with them (Tandon et al., 2012). The most robust support for increased levels of physical activity in children are from parents who both understand children's need to be physically active and provide support and opportunities for play. Encouraging, rather than prohibiting, children to engage in physical activity at home has been found to increase children's level of physical activity (Loprinzi & Trost, 2010). In addition, having a basketball hoop at home (Tandon et al., 2014), providing a variety of play equipment, and engaging in active play with children (Gunter, Rice, Ward, & Trost, 2012) are all associated with higher levels of physical activity in children.

Conclusion

Parents are in a unique position to support children's optimal physical development through parenting practices aimed at developing healthy eating and lifestyle habits. The increasing availability and use of screen time by children can have deleterious effects on their physical activity, sleeping habits, and caloric intake if consumed in excess without parental monitoring. Research supports the use of authoritative parenting practices—high on both demandingness and responsiveness—to facilitate children's self-regulation of food intake as well as their engagement in physical activity and screen time. In relation to food and physical activity, research supports authoritative parenting that includes limiting but not forbidding certain foods and supporting children's physical activity, especially at home. Screen time research suggests that parents should both place limits on screen time and talk to their children about why those limits are important. Psychologists may use the Parent Development Theory (PDT) to help discuss with parents developmentally appropriate strategies to use with their children in order to foster healthy physical development.

References

Adachi-Mejia, A. M., Longacre, M. R., Gibson, J. J., Beach, M. L., Titus-Ernstoff, L. T., & Dalton, M. A. (2006). Children with a TV in their bedroom at higher risk for being overweight. *International Journal of Obesity 4*(31) 644-651. doi:10.1038/sj.ijo.0803455

Adamo, K. B., Wilson, S., Belanger, K., & Chaput, J. P. (2013). Later bedtime is associated with greater daily energy intake and screen time in obese adolescents independent of sleep duration. *Journal of Sleep Disorders & Therapy, 2*(126), 2167-0277. doi:10.4172/2167-0277.1000126

American Academy of Pediatrics, Council on Communications and Media (2013). Policy Statement: Children, Adolescents, and the Media. *Pediatrics, 132*(5), 958-961. doi:10. 1542/peds. 2013-2656.

Baumrind, D. (1971). Current patterns of parental authority. *Developmental Psychology, 4*(1, Pt. 2), 1-103.

Baumrind, D. (2005). Patterns of parental authority and adolescent autonomy. *New Directions For Child and Adolescent Development, 2005*(108), 61-69.

Benton, D. (2004). Role of parents in the determination of the food preferences of children and the development of obesity. *International Journal of Obesity, 28*, 858-869.

Birch, L. L., Birch, D., Marlin, D. W., & Kramer, L. (1982). Effects of instrumental consumption on children's food preference. *Appetite, 3*(2), 125-134.

Birch, L. L., Fisher, J. O., & Davison, K. K. (2003). Learning to overeat: Maternal use of restrictive feeding practices promotes girls' eating in the absence of hunger. *American Journal of Clinical Nutrition, 78*(2), 215-220.

Birch, L. L., Fisher, J. O., Grimm-Thomas, K., Markey, C. N., Sawyer, R., & Johnson, S. L. (2001). Confirmatory factor analysis of the Child Feeding Questionnaire: A measure of parental attitudes, beliefs and practices about child feeding and obesity proneness. *Appetite, 36*, 201-210.

Birch, L. L., Marlin, D., & Rotter, J. (1984). Eating as the means activity in a contingency: Effects on young children's food preference. *Child Development, 55*, 432-439.

Birch, L. L., McPhee, L., Shoba, B. C., Steinberg, L., & Krehbiel, R. (1987). "Clean up your plate": Effects of child feeding practices on the conditioning of meal size. *Learning and Motivation, 18*, 301-317.

Black, M., & Aboud, F. E. (2011). Responsive feeding is embedded in a theoretical framework of responsive parenting. *The Journal of Nutrition, 141*(3), 490-494.

Buijzen, M. (2009). The effectiveness of parental communication in modifying the relation between food advertising and children's consumption behaviour. *British Journal of Developmental Psychology, 27*(1), 105-121.

Buijzen, M., Shuurman, J., & Bomhof, E. (2008). Associations between children's television advertising exposure and their food consumption patterns: A household diary-survey study. *Appetite, 50*, 231-239.

Carlson, S. A., Fulton, J. E., Lee, S. M., Foley, J. T., Heitzler, C., & Huhman, M. (2010). Influence of limit-setting and participation in physical activity on youth screen time. *Pediatrics, 126*(1), 89-96. doi:10.1542/peds.2009-3374

Chamberlain, L. J., Wang, Y., & Robinson, T. N. (2006). Does children's screen time predict requests for advertised products?: Cross-sectional and prospective analyses. *Archives of Pediatrics & Adolescent Medicine, 160*(4), 363. doi:10.1001/archpedi.160.4.363

Council on Sports Medicine and Fitness and Council on School Health. (2006). Active healthy living: Prevention of childhood obesity through increased physical activity. *Pediatrics, 117*(5), 1834-1842.

Daniels, S. (2006). The consequences of childhood overweight and obesity. *The Future of Children, 16*(1), 47-67.

de Jong, E., Stocks, T., Visscher, T. L. S., HiraSing, R. A., Seidell, J. C., & Renders, C. M. (2012). Association between sleep duration and overweight: The importance of parenting. *International Journal of Obesity, 36*(10), 1278-1284. doi:10.1038/ijo.2012.119

de Jong, E., Visscher, T. L. S., Hirasing, R. A., Heymans, M. W., Seidell, J. C., & Renders, C. M. (2011). Association between TV viewing, computer use and overweight, determinants and competing activities of screen time in 4- to 13-year-old children. *International Journal of Obesity, 37*(1), 47-53.

Dennison, B. A., Erb, T. A., & Jenkins, P. L. (2002). Television viewing and television in bedroom associated with overweight risk among low-income preschool children. *Pediatrics, 109*(6), 1028-1035. doi:10.1542/peds.109.6.1028

De Onis, M., Blossner, M., & Borghi, E. (2010). Global prevalence and trends of overweight and obesity among preschool children. *The American Journal of Clinical Nutrition, 92*, 1257-1264.

Drescher, A. A., Goodwin, J. L., Silva, G. E., & Quan, S. F. (2011). Caffeine and screen time in adolescence: Associations with short sleep and obesity. *Journal of Clinical Sleep Medicine, 7*(4), 337-342. doi:10.5664/JCSM.1182

Faith, M. S., Scanlon, K. S., Birch, L. L., Francis, L. A., & Sherry, B. (2004). Parent-child feeding strategies and their relationships to child eating and weight status. *Obesity Research, 12*(11), 1711-1722.

Faith, M. S., Storey, M., Kral, T. V. E., & Pietrobelli, A. (2008). The Feeding Demands Questionnaire: Assessment of parental demand cognitions concerning parent-child feeding relations. *Journal of the American Dietetic Association, 108*(4), 624-630.

Fisher, J. O., & Birch, L. L. (1999). Restricting access to a palatable food affects children's behavioral response, food selection and intake. *American Journal of Clinical Nutrition, 69*, 1264-1272.

Fisher, J. O., Mitchell, D. C., Smiciklas-Wright, H., & Birch, L. L. (2002). Parental influences on young girls' fruit and vegetable, micronutrient, and fat intakes. *Journal of the American Dietetic Association, 102*(1), 58-64.

FitzPatrick, E., Edmunds, L. S., & Dennison, B. A. (2007). Positive effects of family dinner are undone by television viewing. *Journal of the American Dietetic Association, 107*(4), 666-671. doi:10.1016/j.jada.2007.01.014

Galloway, A. T., Fiorito, L. M., Francis, L. A., & Birch, L. L. (2006). "Finish your soup": Counterproductive effects of pressuring children to eat on intake and affect. *Appetite, 46*, 318-323.

Gevers, D. W. M., Kremers, S. P. J., de Vries, N. K., & van Assema, P. (2014). Clarifying concepts of food parenting practices: A Delphi study with an application to snacking behavior. *Appetite, 79*, 51-57.

Gunter, K. B., Rice, K. R., Ward, D. S., & Trost, S. G. (2012). Factors associated with physical activity in children attending family child care homes. *Preventive Medicine, 54*(2), 131-133. doi:10.1016/j.ypmed.2011.12.002

Hale, L., Berger, L. M., LeBourgeois, M. K., & Brooks-Gunn, J. (2011). A longitudinal study of preschoolers' language-based bedtime routines, sleep duration, and well-being. *Journal of Family Psychology, 25*(3), 423.

Halford, J. C. G., Boyland, E. J., Hughes, G., Oliveira, L. P., & Dovey, T. M. (2007). Beyond-brand effect of television (TV) food advertisements/commercials on caloric intake and food choice of 5–7-year-old children. *Appetite, 49*(1), 263-267. doi:10.1016/j.appet.2006.12.003

Hays, J., Power, T. G., & Olvera, N. (2001). Effects of maternal socialization strategies on children's nutrition knowledge and behavior. *Journal of Applied Developmental Psychology, 22*(4), 421-437.

Hindman, A. H., & Morrison, F. J. (2011). Family involvement and educator outreach in Head Start: Nature, extent, and contributions to early literacy skills. *The Elementary School Journal, 111*(3), 359-386. doi:10.1086/657651

Hoerr, S. L., Hughes, S. O., Fisher, J. O., Nicklas, T. A., Liu, Y., & Shewchuk, R. M. (2009). Associations among parental feeding styles and children's food intake in families with limited incomes. *International Journal of Behavioral Nutrition and Physical Activity, 6*, 55-62.

Hubbs-Tait, L., Kennedy, T. S., Page, M. C., Topham, G. L., & Harrist, A. W. (2008). Parental feeding practices predict authoritative, authoritarian, and permissive parenting styles. *Journal of the American Dietetic Association, 108*, 1154-1161.

Hughes, S. O., Power, T. G., Fisher, J. O., Mueller, S., & Nicklas, T. A. (2005). Revisiting a neglected construct: Parenting styles in a child-feeding context. *Appetite, 44*, 83-92.

Hughes, S. O., Shewchuk, R. M., Baskin, M. L., Nicklas, T. A., & Qu, H. (2008). Indulgent feeding style and children's weight status in preschool. *Journal of Developmental and Behavioral Pediatrics, 29*(5), 403-410.

Janssen, I., Craig, W. M., Boyce, W. F., & Pickett, W. (2004). Associations between overweight and obesity with bullying behaviors in school-aged children. *Pediatrics, 113*(5), 1187-1194.

Langer, S. L., Crain, A. L., Senso, M. M., Levy, R. L., & Sherwood, N. E. (2014). Predicting child physical activity and screen time: Parental support for physical activity and general parenting styles. *Journal of Pediatric Psychology, 39*(6), 633-642. doi:10.1093/jpepsy/jsu021

Larson, N. I., Neumark-Sztainer, D., Hannan, P. J., & Story, M. (2007). Family meals during adolescence are associated with higher diet quality and healthful meal patterns during young adulthood. *Journal of the American Dietetic Association, 107*(9), 1502-1510. doi:10.1016/j.jada.2007.06.012

Laurson, K. R., Lee, J. A., Gentile, D. A., Walsh, D. A., & Eisenmann, J. C. (2014). Concurrent associations between physical activity, screen time, and sleep duration with childhood obesity. *ISRN Obesity, 2014*, 1-6. doi:10.1155/2014/204540

Lee, Y., Mitchell, D. C., Smiciklas-Wright, H., & Birch, L. L. (2001). Diet quality, nutrient intake, weight status and feeding environment of girls meeting or exceeding recommendations for total dietary fat of the American Academy of Pediatrics. *Pediatrics, 107*(6), 95.

Lissau, I., & Sorensen, T. I. (1994). Parental neglect during childhood and increased risk of obesity in young adulthood. *Lancet, 343*, 324-327.

Loprinzi, P. D., & Trost, S. G. (2010). Parental influences on physical activity behavior in preschool children. *Preventive Medicine, 50*(3), 129-133. doi:10.1016/j.ypmed.2009.11.010

Maccoby, E., & Martin, J. (1983). Socialization in the context of the family: Parent-child interaction. In E. Hetherington (Ed.), *Handbook of child psychology: Socialization, personality and social development* (pp. 1-101). New York, NY: Wiley.

Malik, V. S., Pan, A., Willett, W. C., & Hu, F. B. (2013). Sugar-sweetened beverages and weight gain in children and adults: a systematic review and meta-analysis. *American Journal of Clinical Nutrition, 98*(4), 1084-1102. http://doi.org/10.3945/ajcn.113.058362

Mark, A. E., & Janssen, I. (2008). Relationship between screen time and metabolic syndrome in adolescents. *Journal of Public Health, 30*(2), 153-160. doi:10.1093/pubmed/fdn022

Mayo Clinic. (2013, August 16). Children and TV: Limiting your child's screen time. *mayoclinic.org*. Retrieved from http://www.mayoclinic.org/healthy-lifestyle/childrens-health/in-depth/children-and-tv/art-20047952?pg=1

Miller, S. A., Taveras, E. M., Rifas-Shiman, S. L., & Gillman, M. W. (2008). Association between television viewing and poor diet quality in young children. *International Journal of Pediatric Obesity, 3*(3), 168-176. doi:10.1080/17477160801915935

Mowder, B. A. (2005). Parent Development Theory: Understanding parents, parenting perceptions and parenting behaviors. *Journal of Early Childhood and Infant Psychology, 1*, 45-64.

National Sleep Foundation. (2014, March 3). National Sleep Foundation 2014 Sleep in America poll finds children sleep better when parents establish rules, limit technology and set a good example. *sleepfoundation.org*. Retrieved from http://sleepfoundation.org/media-center/press-release/national-sleep-foundation-2014-sleep-america-poll-finds-children-sleep

NICHD Early Child Care Research Network (Ed.). (2005). *Child care and child development: Results from the NICHD study of early child care and youth development*. New York, NY: Guildford Press.

O'Connor, T. M., Chen, T. A., Baranowski, J., Thompson, D., & Baranowski, T. (2013). Physical activity and screen-media-related parenting practices have different associations with children's objectively measured physical activity. *Childhood Obesity, 9*(5), 446-453. doi:10.1089/chi.2012.0131

O'Connor, T. M., Hughes, S. O., Watson, K. B., Baranowski, T., Nicklas, T. A., Fisher, J. O., . . . Shewchuk, R. M. (2010). Parenting practices are associated with fruit and vegetable consumption in pre-school children. *Public Health Nutrition, 13*(1), 91-101. doi:10.1018/S1368980009005916

Ogden, C. L., Carroll, M. D., Kit, B. K., & Flegal, K. M. (2012). Prevalence of obesity and trends in body mass index among US children and adolescents, 1999-2010. *Journal of the American Medical Association, 307*(5), 483-490.

Outley C, Taddese A. (2006). A content analysis of health and physical activity messages marketed to African American children during after-school television programming. *Arch Pediatr Adolesc Med*.2006;160(4):432-435. doi:10.1001/archpedi.160.4.432.

Patrick, H., Nicklas, T. A., Hughes, S. O., & Morales, M. (2005). The benefits of authoritative feeding style: Caregiver feeding styles and children's food consumption patterns. *Appetite, 44*, 243-249.

Rhee, K. E., Lumeng, J. C., Appugliese, D. P., Kaciroti, N., & Bradley, R. H. (2006). Parenting styles and overweight status in first grade. *Pediatrics, 117*(6), 2047-2054.

Robinson, C. C., Mandleco, B., Olsen, S. F., & Hart, C. H. (2001). The Parenting Styles and Dimensions Questionnaire (PSDQ). In B. F. Perlmutter, J. Touliatos, & G. W. Holden (Eds.), *Handbook of Family Measurement Techniques: Instruments & Index* (Vol. 3, pp. 319-321). Thousand Oaks, CA: Sage.

Satter, E. M. (1986). The feeding relationship. *Journal of the American Dietetic Association, 86*(3), 352-356.

Stahl, C. E., Necheles, J. W., Mayefsky, J. H., Wright, L. K., & Rankin, K. M. (2011). 5-4-3-2-1 go!: Coordinating pediatric resident education and community health promotion to address the obesity epidemic in children and youth. *Clinical Pediatrics, 50*(3), 215-224. doi:10.1177/0009922810385106

Steele, R. M., van Sluijs, E. M., Cassidy, A., Griffin, S. J., & Ekelund, U. (2009). Targeting sedentary time or moderate- and vigorous-intensity activity: Independent relations with adiposity in a population-based sample of 10-y-old British children. *American Journal of Clinical Nutrition, 90*(5), 1185-1192. doi:10.3945/ajcn.2009.28153

Tandon, P., Grow, H. M., Couch, S., Glanz, K., Sallis, J. F., Frank, L. D., & Saelens, B. E. (2014). Physical and social home environment in relation to children's overall and home-based physical activity and sedentary time. *Preventive Medicine, 66*, 39-44. doi:10.1016/j.ypmed.2014.05.019

Tandon, P. S., Zhou, C., Sallis, J. F., Cain, K. L., Frank, L. D., & Saelens, B. E. (2012). Home environment relationships with children's physical activity, sedentary time, and screen time by socioeconomic status. *International Journal of Behavioral Nutrition and Physical Activity, 9*(88), 1-9.

Taveras, E. M. (2011). Randomized controlled trial to improve primary care to prevent and manage childhood obesity: The high five for kids study. *Archives of Pediatrics & Adolescent Medicine, 165*(8), 714. doi:10.1001/archpediatrics.2011.44

Van Cauter, E., & Knutson, K. L. (2008). Sleep and the epidemic of obesity in children and adults. *European Journal of Endocrinology, 159*, 59-66. doi:10.1530/EJE-08-0298

Ventura, A. K., & Birch, L. L. (2008). Does parenting affect children's eating and weight status? *International Journal of Behavioral Nutrition and Physical Activity, 5*(1), 1-12. doi:10.1186/1479-5868-5-15

Wansink, B. (2002). Changing eating habits on the home front: Lost lessons from World War II research. *Journal of Public Policy & Marketing, 21*(1), 90-99.

Wardle, J., & Carnell, S. (2007). Parental feeding practices and children's weight. *Acta Paediatrica, 96*, 5-11.

Whitaker, R. C., Wright, J. A., Pepe, M. S., Seidel, K. D., & Dietz, W. H. (1997). Predicting obesity in young adulthood from childhood and parental obesity. *The New England Journal of Medicine, 337*(13), 869-873. doi:10.1056/NEJM199709253371301

Wiecha, J. L., Peterson, K. E., Ludwig, D. S., Kim, J., Sobol, A., & Gortmaker, S. L. (2006). When children eat what they watch: Impact of television viewing on dietary intake in youth. *Archives of Pediatrics & Adolescent Medicine, 160*(4), 436. doi:10.1001/archpedi.160.4.436

Williams, J., Wake, M., Hesketh, K., Maher, E., & Waters, E. (2005). Health-related quality of life of overweight and obese children. *Journal of the American Medical Association, 293*(1), 70-76.

Zheng, M., Rangan, A., Olsen, N. J., Andersen, L. B., Wedderkopp, N., Kristensen, P., . . . Heitmann, B. L. (2014). Substituting sugar-sweetened beverages with water or milk is inversely associated with body fatness development from childhood to adolescence. *Nutrition, 31*(1), 38-44. doi:10.1016/j.nut.2014.04.017

Screen Time Questionnaire: Measuring Parents' and Children's Media Use

Linda Olszewski, Shagufta Asar, Ashley Bogatch, and Alixandra Blackman

Abstract

The use of screened technology has become pertinent when considering parenting. Although television has long been an influence in the homes of Americans, new advances in technology have created more accessible and portable devices, making the study of screen time an area of vital importance. Noting the lack of psychometrically sound instruments in the literature for understanding screen time in the role of parent-child relationships, the authors developed the Screen Time Questionnaire. The development and revision of the Screen Time Questionnaire is discussed.

Key words: children, parents, screen time, questionnaire, measurement

Introduction

In today's society, the topic of screen time is extremely relevant, specifically when considering an early childhood population. Screen time is the exposure to screened media devices, which include computers, hand-held digital devices, smartphones, television, and video games (Mayo Clinic, 2013). Many of these devices are portable and therefore are available 24 hours a day, seven days a week. Starting at young ages, children are exposed to all types of electronic devices. New technologies are evolving at an unprecedented rate and are then quickly integrated into American culture, posing daunting challenges to parents and researchers.

Questions involving screen time's impact on children's development have been asked since the introduction of motion pictures. Some experts viewed the decision to allow children to attend the cinema as one of many "parental failures" (Russell, 1930, p. 69). However, this did not deter many parents from allowing their children to watch films. With the advent of the television in 1939, the idea of having a visual entertainment device in the home was well accepted by Americans and, by 1945, 7,000 homes across America owned one (Goldfarb et al., 2012). Since 1945, there has been a boom in television ownership; according to Nielsen's (2014) Advance National TV Household Universe Estimate (UE), there are reported to be 116.3 million homes that own at least one television, and ownership is on the rise.

Indeed, American families embraced the television despite the contrary view of experts. Classic longitudinal studies looking at the viewing of violent television content found strong correlations between the quantity of television violence viewed at the age of 8 and aggressive behavior at the age of 19 in boys (Eron, Huesmann, Lefkowitz, & Walker, 1972). More recent literature also reports negative associations between television viewing and child outcomes (Anderson, Economos, & Must, 2008; Christiakis & Zimmerman, 2006, 2007). For example, several studies have demonstrated correlations between the amount of television viewed and cognitive delays, speech delays, aggressive behavior, decreased academic performance, attention problems, hyperactivity, irregular sleep patterns, and obesity (Anderson et al., 2008; Christakis & Zimmerman, 2006, 2007; Christakis, Zimmerman, DiGiuseppe, & McCarthy, 2004; Crespo et al., 2001; Pagani, Fitzpatrick, Barnett, & Dubow, 2010).

Educational aspects associated with prolonged screen time use include poor homework completion, poor attitudes toward school, and long-term academic failure (Johnson, Brook, Cohen, & Kasen, 2007). One study found that violent television viewing during preschool was associated with antisocial behavior in school-aged children (Ferguson & Rueda, 2010). The research also demonstrates that some cultural groups are at greater risk with regard to screen time exposure; these include populations with low socio-economic status, African Americans, and Latinos (Rideout, 2011).

Today, screened media goes far beyond television. Hand-held digital devices such as computers, smartphones, tablets, and video games are no longer new phenomenon, and like the television, many American families embrace these technologies, using them as babysitters and calming devices for children. The acceptance and popularity of these devices becomes abundantly clear when reading print media. Technology expert Katie Linendoll "[calls] the iPad the ultimate babysitter.... Because it is very easy to use [and] there's no manual" (Silver, 2011). De Lacey (2012) suggests that mothers are using screened technology as a way to soothe their children in place of using a pacifier.

Mobile applications (apps), which are software designed to function on a mobile device such as a smartphone or a tablet (Janssen, 2014), have become increasingly popular. New research suggests that 89% of smartphone users' time on the device is spent using apps, suggesting that traditional use of the phone is a minimal activity when considering these devices (Nielsen, 2014). Apps have become very popular among parents and children alike. Parents have reported that one-third of the apps on their phone have been downloaded by their children (Nielsen, 2011).

While there may be some immediate, positive effects for toddlers using apps, such as providing a "break" for the parent, averting a tantrum, and perhaps engaging fine-motor skills as toddlers learn to navigate and manipulate the devices, many questions remain about screened technology and its relationship to young children's development. Though screened devices are no longer in their infancy as a technology, a gap exists in the literature as to their effects on young children.

The first three years of life are a period of amazing growth in all areas of children's cognitive, physical, and social-emotional development. The American Academy of Pediatrics (AAP) took a strong stance in 1999 and in 2011 by discouraging parents from allowing children under 2 years of age to watch television at all. The AAP cited research showing that this media has adverse effects on health and developmental outcomes in children younger than 2. The research reveals that screen time has been shown to be positively correlated with aggressive behaviors, attention issues, sleep issues, and obesity in children ages 4 to 18 (AAP, 1999; AAP "Media Education", 2011; Nunez-Smith, Wolf, Huang, Emanuel, & Gross, 2008).

Not all research on screen time indicates negative outcomes for children. In fact, some positive benefits have been found, including educational, cognitive, and language learning benefits. Specifically, individuals with greater video game exposure may demonstrate an improvement in critical thinking skills, problem solving abilities, visual-spatial abilities, and working memory (Prot, McDonald, Anderson, & Gentile, 2012). More prevalent, however, is research highlighting the negative implications of screen time.

With these findings, it becomes important to explore how much time children are engaged in screen-related activities. Some research suggests that the average child under the age of 2 is watching one to two hours of television per day (Zimmerman, Christakis, & Meltzoff, 2007), with marketing that targets these children beginning as early as 4 months of age (Storey & French, 2004). However, if the concept of "media multitasking," using several electronic devices at the same time, is taken into account, the number of hours of exposure for children under the age of 2 increases to 8.5 hours of screen time daily (Roberts & Foehr, 2008). By 3 years of age, 29% of children have a television in their bedroom (Rideout, 2011). This is significant since children are likely engaging in unsupervised screen time with the ability to make programming choices that may be inappropriate for their age. Furthermore, watching television without parental supervision results in lost moments for parent-child interaction or educational opportunities. Research supports this with findings that suggest that having a television that is on and audible is correlated with reduced parent-child interaction (Christakis, Gilkerson, & Richards, 2009).

Another component of screen time is a concept identified as "background screen time," or children's indirect exposure to screened media. For instance, a child may be sitting in a room playing while his or her parents are sitting in the same room watching television that is intended for the adults. Screened media results in parents' attention being diverted from their children to the screen; as such, there is a reduction in active parent-child interaction (Schmidt, Pempek, Kirkorian, Frankenfield, & Anderson, 2008). Furthermore, children may be exposed to age-inappropriate content when a parent is watching programming in their presence that is intended for an adult.

Televisions are not the only source of background screen time; mobile devices are also contributors. Emergency room physicians are expressing concern about mobile devices, suggesting that they serve as high-tech distracters. These doctors propose that parents distracted by hand-held technology may be to blame for the increase in emergency room visits of young children (Worthen, 2012).

On a positive note, some parenting behaviors have been identified as a moderating factor, reducing the negative aspects associated with screen time in children (Bergh et al., 2014; van Lippevelde et al., 2014). For example, if parents communicate with their children about what they are watching on television, the negative effects of background screen time on children may be reduced (Pempek, Kirkorian, & Anderson, 2010). This finding can help psychologists focus on parenting behaviors in early childhood that serve as a protective factor with regard to screen time, which may in turn result in positive relational outcomes for children and parents.

As proliferation and acceptance of hand-held devices in the daily life of parents and caretakers increase along with the increase in children's exposure to these devices, the importance of understanding how screens can affect young children's psychological development is highlighted. A recent study by Carli et al. (2014)

identified children's non-school/work-related screen time as an "invisible risk" factor for psychopathology. Although this study was conducted with adolescents, it emphasizes the importance of investigating the role screens play in the development of young children. How does exposure to screened media relate to a child's academic performance, activity levels, sleep patterns, social and emotional development, and weight? With the advent of the computer and portable screened devices, questions regarding technologies have arisen that have not yet been fully answered.

A literature review reveals that screen time primarily has been measured through the use of daily logs of study-specific measures developed for the purpose of the particular study for which they have been utilized (Aires et al., 2010; Danielsen et al., 2011; Elder et al., 2012; Steele, Richardson, Daratha, & Bindler, 2012). Additionally, the review of scientific research indicates that, to date, a formal measure to determine children's screen time exposure in a valid and reliable manner does not exist. Furthermore, much of the research conducted with regard to screen time has qualified the use of only computers, electronic games, and televisions. With new technology, computers and television screens are slowly being replaced with portable devices such as tablets and smartphones.

If screen time is defined as exposure to all screened media, time spent using smartphones must be included in addition to time spent using computers, televisions, and video games. It is important for the definition of screen time to be operationalized so that it is viewed in a consistent manner across studies. Furthermore, different methods of measuring screen time result in the inability to reliably compare findings across studies. The lack of a standardized method of measuring screen time has been a limitation in the research literature to date.

Development of the Screen Time Questionnaire

After a review of the literature, researchers at the Parent-Child Institute at Pace University recognized the importance of screen time on the parent-child relationship (Jago et al., 2014; Nielsen, 2011). The Screen Time Questionnaire (STQ) was developed by the authors of this article with the purpose of providing researchers with a psychometrically sound instrument for measuring screen time. The ultimate goal is to provide an improved understanding of the associations between screen time and various aspects of child development. Additionally, the STQ takes into account the parent-child relationship, thereby considering the child in a more holistic manner.

A review of the literature revealed that self-reports employed in screen time-related studies often did not include demographic inquiries (Bajovic, 2012; Carli et al., 2014). The creators of the demographic portion of the STQ aimed to include a variety of qualitative factors that could potentially be associated with screen time use (e.g., ethnicity, household income, marital status, parent age, parent educational level). Developing items for the screen time section posed a challenge. Due to the limited research on screen time, specifically research including the use of multiple electronic devices, the authors initially developed questions using a combination of the little research that was available as well as their hypotheses regarding screen time and the parenting relationship. Understanding that parent screen time affects children's screen time habits (Gentile, Reimer, Nathanson, Walsh, & Eisenmann, 2014; Jago et al., 2014; Nielsen, 2011), the parent development theory (PDT) (Mowder, 2005) was used as a theoretical framework for considering the definition of parents and parenting for the STQ. The PDT, having its foundation in cognitive behavioral and social learning theories, looks at parenting as a social role; in other words, parents are the individuals that children perceive as performing certain caretaking functions. The PDT takes into account factors that influence an individual's perception of parenting and how parenting evolves over time, accounting for children's age, evolving needs, parent characteristics, parent-child interactions, family dynamics, and cultural issues. The authors of this article interpreted cultural issues to include social developments and environmental issues (e.g., technological advances). Since the STQ is designed for caretakers to fill out as well as parents, the authors believe it is important to provide a definition of this role. A caretaker, as defined by these researchers, is an individual who is engaged in caring for and supervising a child for 20 hours or more each week; this individual may or may not live with the index child. This definition includes both paid caretakers and non-paid caretakers (e.g., an aunt, a friend, a grandparent, an uncle). The authors also included an extensive demographic section in order to allow researchers to examine screen time in relation to other factors (e.g., child age, parent age, education, employment status, ethnicity, gender, socioeconomic status, marital status).

The STQ was designed to have two distinct sections: a demographic section and a screen time section. These sections are further divided. The demographic section is divided into two parts: the first part asks participants (parents or caretakers) to answer questions about their own demographic information (Part I) and the next part asks participants to answer questions about one child's demographic information (Part II). A screen time portion follows the demographic portion of the STQ, and it is divided into three sections: parent screen time use (Section I), child screen time use (Section II), and parent/child screen time interaction (Section III).

Initial questions were conceptualized in a small focus group consisting of three parents. The following question was posed to the focus group, "What type of screened media do you use?" This question was based on a review of the literature (AAP, 1999; AAP "Media Education", 2011; Aires et al., 2010; Anderson et al., 2008; Christakis & Zimmerman, 2006, 2007; Crespo et al., 2001 Elder et al.,

2012; Gentile et al., 2014; Jago et al., 2014; Mowder, 2005; Nielsen, 2011; Prot et al., 2012). Initial questions included general questions inquiring about both parent and child screen time use (e.g., for both parents and children, questions were asked as follows: How many hours of electronic device usage per day are dedicated to work-related activities? [For children, the word "work-related" is substituted with "educational" in this question.] On average, how many hours of electronic device usage per day are spent on entertainment?)

Next, individual interviews were conducted with 10 parents and caretakers of children between the ages of 6 months and 16 years who had experience with technology in order to further refine questions. For example, the question "How many hours per day are dedicated to work activities?" was reworded to include "school-related activities" as parents in the focus group pointed out that it is possible for parents to simultaneously be students. The question "On average, how many hours *per day* does your child engage in traditional educational activities, *not* using electronic devices?" was elaborated to include examples (e.g., reading stories, learning the alphabet/counting, learning to read, etc.) to make the question more easily understood. Next, existing questions were refined and condensed in accordance with the existing literature; for example, questions were developed that sought information about general screen time use (e.g., How many hours *per day* do you spend using electronic devices?), more specific usage (e.g., On average, how many hours of electronic device usage *per day* are spent on entertainment/leisure [i.e., movies, TV, reading a book on a tablet, social media]? On average, how many hours *per day* do you spend texting?), and background screen time exposure (e.g., On average, how many hours *per day* does your child engage in independent play using traditional toys/activities while sitting in front of a TV that is on?) (AAP, 1999; AAP, "Media Education" 2011; Christakis et al., 2009; Elder et al., 2012; Gentile et al., 2014; Jago et al., 2014; Nielsen, 2011; Prot et al., 2012).

Based on focus group responses, prior research regarding screen time, and consideration of parenting theory (e.g., PDT), three distinct areas of screen time emerged: parent use, child use, and parent/child interaction (i.e., parent and child engaging in screen time together). This differentiation was an important step in structuring the measure and guiding the question development. Once the measure mirrored theory, questions were created to follow the three-part organization of the measure that asks parents about their screen time at home, at work, and on different devices (e.g., computer, smartphone, tablet, video game); asks parents to report their children's screen time at home, at school, during a variety of different activities, and on different devices (e.g., computer, smartphone, tablet, video game); and finally, asks parents to report their screen time in relation to their parenting behavior, such as by asking how much time they engage with their children while using an electronic device. It was essential to the creators of the STQ that they create a user-friendly measure with literature-based and theory-driven (e.g., PDT) questions. Based on research (Aires et al., 2010, Elder et al., 2012), STQ developers decided that each question would have a weekday and a weekend component in order to more precisely assess screen time exposure that varied during weekdays as compared to during the weekend. Additionally, for the ease of use, the meaning of "electronic device" was defined for the individual who administers the questionnaire in the STQ's instructions as follows: "When asking about the use of electronic devices, we mean this to include: TV, Computers, Smart-phones, Tablets, E-readers, MP3 players, Video Game Systems, Handheld DVD players, or any other electronic device used for entertainment purposes."

Initial Structure of the STQ

At the time of its initial development, the STQ consisted of a demographic section, parent screen time use section, child screen time use section, and parent/child interaction section. The demographic section was further divided into two sections: parent demographic information and child demographic information. The parent demographic section included questions about the parent's or caretaker's age, devices owned (e.g., cellular phone, MP3 player, smartphone, tablet, television, video game console), education, employment status, ethnicity, gender, household income, marital status, mental health, and physical health. The child demographic section included questions about the child's age, devices owned (e.g., cellular phone, MP3 player, smartphone, television, tablet, video game console), gender, mental health, and physical health.

In the three screen time sections, respondents were asked to circle a number corresponding to the time they spent using screened devices daily (0, 1, 2, 3, ... 22, 23, 24 hours), rounding up to the nearest hour. Section I, parent screen time use, included 11 questions related to parent screen time (e.g., On average, how many hours *per day* do you spend using electronic devices? On average, how many hours per day do you spend actively watching TV?).

Section II, child screen time use, was comprised of 17 questions, some of which inquired about the child's screened media usage (e.g., On average, how many hours per day does your child engage in independent play/activities using electronic devices [e.g., video games, movies, shows, etc.]? On average, how many hours per day does your child engage in play with a friend using electronic entertainment devices?) The child section also included questions about traditional play activities (e.g., On average, how many hours per day does your child engage in play with a friend using traditional toys or imagination? On average, how many hours per day does your child engage in traditional educational activities [e.g., reading stories, learning the alphabet/counting, learning to read] not using electronic devices?) Additionally, the child section included one multiple–part qualitative question in which parents were asked to rate the amount of time they use devices to calm or occupy their child (e.g., How often is your smartphone or other electronic device used to calm/occupy your child in the following settings: Grocery Store, Running Errands, In the car, While doing chores at home, To put your child to bed) on a four-point, Likert-type scale (i.e., Never, Sometimes, Often, Always).

Section III, parent/child screen time interaction, was comprised of four questions and included questions about parent and child interaction and engagement in screened media (e.g., On average, how many hours per day spent on electronic devices are also spent engaged with your child [i.e., playing games together, watching TV together, reading a book together]? On average, how many hours per day spent on electronic devices are not spent engaged with your child [i.e., at work, in a different room, in the same room working on different activities]? Are any electronic devices on in the background during dinner?)

An additional three questions were added on at the end of the questionnaire to determine if any devices were overlooked by the authors, as well as to determine which devices were most used (i.e., Are there any electronic devices that you use for entertainment purposes that we didn't include in this survey? On which devices are video games most often played? On which devices are TV shows or movies most often watched?). Finally, a feedback section was included at the end of the survey to allow for parent feedback regarding the questionnaire (i.e., Please feel free to leave comments, suggestions, or concerns you may have regarding this survey). In sum, a total of 35 questions made up the STQ, excluding the demographic section and the feedback section.

Psychometric Properties of the Original STQ

The STQ's content validity was evidenced by an evaluation of 30 judges, through interviews and discussions, and via comparison with the literature (Aires et al., 2010, Bajovic, 2012 Crespo et al., 2001, Elder et al., 2012; Gentile et al., 2014; Jago et al., 2014; Mowder, 2005; Nielsen, 2011).

The pilot study for the STQ was conducted using the 35-item questionnaire. The purpose of the pilot study was to determine clarity and reliability of the piloted questions of the STQ. Participants consisted of both parents, as defined by the PDT (Mowder, 2005), and caretakers, as defined by these authors, of children aged 0-18. Participants were asked to evaluate their own screen time use as well as the screen time use of a child in their care. The screened device usage in the dyadic relationship and the exposure to background screen time were examined as well. Participants were also requested to provide feedback in order to better develop the questionnaire. The questionnaires were disseminated in-vivo across the five boroughs of New York City and through various websites such as Facebook.

The overall reliability of the original, 35-item questionnaire was found to be acceptable (Cronbach's a = 0.781) based on the sample of 25 participants who met the criteria of being a parent or caretaker of a child aged 0-18, as defined by the PDT (Mowder, 2005) and the authors of the STQ.

Revision of the STQ

Several modifications were made to the STQ based on the initial analysis, feedback from participants, and consultations with professionals in test development. For example, the measurement of time was changed from circling the corresponding number of hours to a fill–in–the–blank format. Questions that had zero variance or low item total correlation were considered and ultimately removed from the questionnaire. Certain questions were also removed due to legality concerns regarding suggested behaviors, such as screen time use while driving. In addition to the removal of questions from the STQ, inquiries were also subtly modified. For example, the question "On average, how many hours of electronic device usage per day are spent on entertainment/leisure (e.g., movies, T.V., reading on a tablet, social media)" was modified as follows (changes are italicized): On average, how many hours of electronic device usage per day are spent on entertainment/leisure (e.g., movies, T.V., reading a *book* on a tablet, social media)? Finally, the scales of measurement for questions were changed in order to maintain consistency throughout the questionnaire. For example, multiple-part questions in the child section were changed from a four-point Likert scale to a fill-in-the-blank format for weekday and weekend time spent on a particular activity (e.g., How often is your smartphone or other electronic device used to calm/occupy your child in the following settings: Grocery Store, Running Errands, In the car, While doing chores at home, To put your child to bed?). An additional question was added (On average, how many hours per day does your child engage in independent play/activities using electronic devices [e.g., video games, movies, shows, applications on hand held devices]?) The purpose of the addition was to ensure a comprehensive questionnaire.

    The revised STQ is similar in construction to the pilot and has a total of 30 questions. The STQ is comprised of a demographic section, which is divided into two parts: the first demographic section concerns parents/caretakers (e.g., age, devices owned, education, employment status, ethnicity, gender, household income, marital status, mental health, and physical health). The second, child demographic, section includes questions about the child's age, devices owned, mental health, and physical health. Prior to proceeding to Section I to answer questions about electronic device usage, the questionnaire provides the parent and/or caretaker with a specific definition of electronic devices to avoid confusion (i.e., Electronic devices include television, MP3 player, cellular phone, smartphone, tablet, video game console, computer, and other devices). Additionally, participants are asked to indicate how many hours, based on a 24-hour day, they and their child engage in various behaviors and are asked to round to the nearest half hour. Finally, the revised STQ provides parents and/or caretakers with the option of checking a box indicating that the question does not apply to them or their child (i.e., N/A).

    Section I, parent's screen time, is made up of nine 2-part questions (weekday use, weekend use) inquiring about the parent/

caretaker's screen time use (e.g., On average, how many hours per day do you spend using electronic devices? On average, how many hours of electronic device usage per day are dedicated to work/school related activities? On average, how many hours per day is your TV on?).

Section II considers child screen time use and is comprised of 14 questions; of these, 11 are two-part questions inquiring about screen time use on weekdays and weekends (e.g., On average, how many hours per day does your child use electronic devices? On average, how many hours per day does your child engage with a friend using electronic entertainment devices [e.g., in play or in conversation]? On average, how many hours per day does your child use electronic devices while in transit [e.g., car, train]? On average, how many hours per day is your smartphone or other electronic device used to calm/occupy your child?) Section II also has three, multiple-part questions that inquire about specific screen time use on weekdays and weekends (e.g., On average, how many hours per day does your child use the following electronic devices for entertainment/leisure purposes? Television [weekday use, weekend use], MP3 player [weekday use, weekend use], Smartphone [weekday use, weekend use], Tablet [weekday use, weekend use], Video game console [weekday use, weekend use], Computer [weekday use, weekend use], Other [weekday use, weekend use]).

Section III, which considers parent/caretaker and child interaction, is comprised of five 2-part questions. Two questions use the fill-in-the-blank format (e.g., On average, how many hours per day spent on electronic devices are also spent engaged with your child [e.g., playing games together, watching TV together, reading a book together, playing a video game]? On average, how many hours per day spent on electronic devices are not spent engaged with your child [e.g., at work, in a different room, in the same room working on different activities]?) The revised STQ includes three additional questions (i.e., On average, how often does your family eat dinner together? How often does your family watch TV while eating dinner together? On average, how often are electronic devices on in the background during dinner?) These questions use a four-point, Likert-type scale (i.e., Never, Sometimes, Often, Always) and are divided into two-part questions inquiring about weekday and weekend usage.

The remaining two questions on the revised STQ are for informational use only (i.e., Are there any electronic devices that you use for work/educational and entertainment purposes that were not included in this survey? On which devices are: a) video games most often played? b) TV shows and movies most often viewed?).

Psychometric Properties of the Revised STQ

Similar to the piloted STQ, content validity of the revised STQ was determined by interviews, discussions, an evaluation by judges, and, finally, with a comparison to relevant literature (Aires et al., 2010, Bajovic, 2012 Crespo et al., 2001; Elder et al., 2012; Gentile et al., 2014; Jago et al., 2014; Mowder, 2005; Nielsen, 2011).

Participants

The sample was comprised of 203 participants. Researchers merged parent and caretaker data in the analysis of the STQ. This consolidation took place and authors viewed parents and caretakers as one entity for the purposes of this study. The authors maintain that parents and caretakers potentially have a similar impact a child's media habits and exposure.

Of the 202 individuals who completed the survey, the mean age of the parent/caretaker was 39.63 and the mean age of the child was 7.24. Female participants comprised 79.3% of the sample and males 20.7%. There were 146 participants identified as Caucasian (71.9%), 21 as Asian/Pacific Islander (10.3%), 10 as Latino (4.9%), six as African American (3.0%), one as American Indian/Alaskan (0.5%), 12 as Multi-Ethnic (5.9%), and six selected Other (3.0%). Additionally, 74 participants reported having an annual household income of $200,001 or more (36.5%), 51 reported having a household income of $101,000–$200,000 (25.1%), 41 reported a household income of $75,001–$100,000 (20.2%), 14 a household income of $50,001–$75,000 (6.9%), nine reported a household income of $25,001–$50,000 (4.4%), and 10 reported a household income of less than $25,000 (4.9%), 3 participants (2.0%) chose not to answer household income information.

Procedure

The questionnaires were again disseminated throughout New York City to both parents and caretakers. Questionnaires were distributed in-vivo in various locations, including preschools, sporting events in the five boroughs of New York City, and public parks. The STQ was also circulated digitally through e-mail groups as well as social media sites such as Facebook and through parenting associations at various public schools. The participants were informed of the voluntary and anonymous nature of their participation.

The total number of surveys collected was 203; of these, two were removed since the age of the child did not meet the study's criteria (ages 0–18). The mean was substituted for missing items. Based on the analysis for this sample of 201 participants, the overall alpha for the questionnaire was found to be high ($\alpha = .86$). Further analysis was completed on the data. However, due to the design of the revised STQ, which is divided into four distinct sections (Demographic section, Section I, Section II, and Section III) with Section I looking only at parent/caretaker screen time and Sections II and III focusing on child screen time use, items were analyzed separately by sections: parent/caretaker screen time use, child screen time use, and parent/caretaker-child interaction. The items were separated into parent/caretaker items (nine items) and child items (14 items) and were analyzed separately.

Results

A principal component analysis (PCA) was conducted on the nine items centered on parent/caretaker screen time with orthogonal rotation (varimax). The Kaiser-Meyer-Olkin measure verified the sampling adequacy for the analysis, KMO = .76 ('good' according to Field, 2009; Hutcheson & Sofroniou, 1999; Kaiser, 1970). Bartlett's test of sphericity, $c^2(201) = 3098.17$, $p = .00$, indicated that correlations between items were sufficiently large for PCA. Five components were found to have eigenvalues over Kaiser's criterion of 1. The scree plot was slightly ambiguous and showed inflections that would justify reducing the components to three factors and in combination explained 63.64% of the variance. Given the convergence of the scree plot, this is the number of components that were retained in the final analysis. Table 1 illustrates the factor loadings after rotation. The items that cluster on the same components suggest that component 1 represents "parent general screen time," component 2 "parental screen distraction," and component 3 "parent overall screen time."

Factor 1, Parent General Screen Time, includes items revolving around electronic device usage, which includes time spent on a cellular phone, texting, viewing television, and engaged with an electronic device and not engaged with the child (i.e., background screen time). Above all, these markers were a more general overview of screen time.

Factor 2, Parental Screen Distraction, has items that inquire about parent electronic device use for entertainment and television viewing. Specifically, questions are related to active hours of television viewing, inactive hours of viewing television, and entertainment/leisure use of electronic devices, all of which can be categorized as background screen time.

Factor 3, Parent Overall Screen Time, is comprised of questions that inquire about overall screen time or hours spent using electronic devices for work and entertainment/leisure purposes.

Table 1:
Factor Loadings, Descriptive and Precision Data of the Parent/Caretaker Scale

	Factor 1: Parent General Screen Time		Factor 2: Parental Screen Distraction		Factor 3: Parent Overall Screen Time	
	Item	Factor Load	Item	Factor Load	Item	Factor Load
	3a.	.430	3a.	.581	1a.	.833
	4a.	.610	3b.	.526	1b.	.619
	4b.	.639	6a.	.883	2a.	.731
	5a.	.788	6b.	.860	2b.	.418
	5b.	.721	7a.	.466	3b.	.493
	7a.	.755	7b.	.448		
	7b.	.709	8a.	.799		
	9a.	.818	8b.	.789		
	9b.	.813				
Var. explained		27.06		23.10		13.39
Cronbach's a		.91		.90		.70

Overall reliability for parent factors reveals a Cronbach's *alpha* demonstrating a high reliability, $a = .91$. Factor 1, "parent general screen time," has a high reliability, Cronbach's $a = .91$. Factor 2, "parent background screen time," has a high reliability, Cronbach's $a = .90$. Factor 3, "parent general screen time," has an adequate reliability, Cronbach's $a = .70$.

A PCA was conducted on the 18 items centered on child screen time ($n = 201$) with orthogonal rotation (varimax). The Kaiser-Meyer-Olkin measure verified the sampling adequacy for the analysis, KMO = .64 ('adequate' according to Field, 2009; Kaiser, 1970). Bartlett's test of sphericity, $c^2(201) = 10656.12$, $p = .00$, indicated that correlations between items were sufficiently large for PCA. An analysis was run to obtain eigenvalues for eight components of the data. Eight components were found to have eigenvalues over Kaiser's criterion of 1 and in combination explained 79.34% of the variance. The scree plot was slightly ambiguous and showed inflections that would justify reducing the components to six. Given the convergence of the scree plot and Kaiser's criterion of six components, the number of components that were retained in the final analysis was six. Table 2 shows the factor loadings after rotation. The items that cluster on the same components suggest that component 1 represents "child general screen time," component 2 "child entertainment/leisure screen time," component 3 "passive screen time," component 4 "child music and gaming screen time," component 5 "traditional play - no screen time," and component 6 represents "child pacifying screen time."

Factor 1, Child General Screen Time, is comprised of questions inquiring about general usage of electronic devices (alone and with a friend) in addition to specific usage habits of a child with regard to smartphones and computers.

Factor 2, Child Entertainment/Leisure Screen Time, is characterized by an entertainment-based usage of electronic devices. Specifically, it inquires about the time a child engages with electronic devices such as a television, tablet, or computer for entertainment purposes (e.g., using electronic devices with parent or while parent is busy).

Factor 3, Passive Screen Time, consists of questions that inquire about a passive usage of electronic devices (e.g., to help settle a child down for bed or a device that is on in the background while the child is engaged in traditional play).

Factor 4, Child Music and Gaming Screen Time, specifically inquires about MP3 player and video game usage, including both educational and entertainment/leisure purposes.

Factor 5, Traditional Play - No Screen Time, asks questions regarding activities that do not involve the use of electronic devices, focusing on traditional play activities (e.g., playing with dolls, playing with a friend or sibling).

Finally, Factor 6, Child Pacifying Screen Time, is comprised of questions inquiring about the pacifying use of devices when running errands or doing chores.

Table 2:
Factor Loadings, Descriptive and Precision Data of the Child Scale

	Factor 1: Child General Screen Time		Factor 2: Child Entertainment/ Leisure Screen Time		Factor 3: Passive Screen Time	
	Item	Factor Load	Item	Factor Load	Item	Factor Load
	10a.	.485	10a.	.570	11a(i).	.712
	10b.	.464	10b.	.548	11a(ii).	.665
	11c(i).	.765	12a(i).	.748	11d(ii).	.721
	11c(ii).	.823	12a(ii).	.499	15b.	.571
	11f(ii).	.713	12d(i).	.539	18c(i).	.750
	12c(i).	.872	12d(ii).	.493	18c(ii)	.779
	12c(ii)	.895	16b.	.428	18e(i)	.766
	13a.	.813	17a.	.633	20a.	.557
	13b.	.835	17b.	.520	20b.	.610
	14a (i)	.691	21a.	.718		
	14b(ii)	.762	21b.	.638		
			24a.	.580		
			24b.	.497		
			25b.	.482		
Var. Explained	11.63		9.49		7.70	
Cronbach's *a*	.910		.869		.805	

(Table 2 continued on next page)

(Table 2 continued from previous page)

Table 2:
Factor Loadings, Descriptive and Precision Data of the Child Scale

	Factor 4: Child Music & Gaming Screen Time		Factor 5: Traditional Play – No Screen Time		Factor 6: Child Pacifying Screen Time	
	Item	Factor Load	Item	Factor Load	Item	Factor Load
	11b(i)	.856	19a(i)	.685	18b(i)	.645
	11b(ii).	.839	19b(ii)	.711	18b(ii)	.684
	11e(i).	.882	22a(ii)	.442	18d(i)	.580
	11e(ii).	.751	23a(i)	.742	18d(ii)	.498
	12b(i).	.503	23a(ii)	.513		
	12b(ii).	.542				
	12e(i).	.689				
	12e(ii).	.635				
Var. Explained		5.22		5.15		4.94
Cronbach's a		.824		.776		.619

Overall reliability for child items reveals a high reliability, Cronbach's a = .86. Factor 1, "general screen time," has a high reliability, Cronbach's a = .91. Factor 2, "child entertainment/leisure screen time," has a high reliability, Cronbach's a = .869. Factor 3, "child passive screen time," has a high reliability, Cronbach's a = .805. Factor 4, "child music and gaming screen time," has a high reliability, Cronbach's a = .824. Factor 5, "child traditional play – no screen time," has an adequate reliability, Cronbach's a = .776 Factor 6, "child pacifying screen time," has an acceptable reliability, Cronbach's a = .619.

The STQ demonstrates promising reliability; however, it continues to require revisions. Administration of the questionnaire must be simplified for the ease of both the administrator and the parent/caretaker being administered the questionnaire. The current fill-in-the-blank format was reported by parents to be difficult and was often unsuccessfully completed by parents and/or caretakers. Similarly, for the administrators, it proved difficult at times to read responses. Future revisions will focus on simplification of measurement, requiring parents/caretakers to answer on a Likert scale of 1 to 5, which will correspond to spans of hours. This will likely facilitate use of the questionnaire for both parents/caretakers as well as administrators of the STQ.

Discussion

When considering an early childhood population, it is clear that screen time is an extremely relevant topic. The exposure to visual electronic devices, including portable devices, has many implications associated with future outcomes for a child. Technologies evolve quickly, making research challenging in this area. Because of the increased amount of screen exposure, technology is taking on an increasingly influential role in the social and cognitive development of children. With the AAP's strong stance discouraging screen time for children under two years of age (AAP, 1999; AAP "Media Use", 2011) and sobering studies demonstrating a correlation between television viewing and cognitive delays, speech delays, aggressive behavior, psychopathology, decreased academic performance, and obesity (Anderson et al., 2008; Carli et al., 2014; Christakis & Zimmerman, 2007; Crespo et al., 2001; Pagani et al., 2010), it is clear that screen time is a crucial topic to continue to research.

In the past, screen time has been primarily measured through the use of daily logs developed specifically for the purpose of one single study (Aires et al., 2010; Danielsen et al., 2011; Elder et al., 2012; Steele et al., 2012). Prior to the STQ, a formal measure to determine screen time among children, particularly young children, did not exist. Measuring screen time in a valid and reliable way is essential to psychologists and to further research in this area. Early childhood is a critical period for assessing screen time and raising parent and caretaker awareness. The evolution of the STQ has been purposed to help assess and understand screen time within this critical period of early childhood. Although it continues to undergo revisions, significant progress has been made in developing and enhancing this measure for use in a variety of capacities. The STQ aims to be a valid and reliable tool that will benefit psychologists and researchers as well as practitioners to help uncloak this "invisible risk" (Carli et al., 2014) by bringing awareness to parents and caretakers and helping psychologists to implement appropriate interventions.

References

Aires, L. L., Andersen, L. B., Mendonça, D. D., Martins, C. C., Silva, G. G., & Mota, J. J. (2010). A 3-year longitudinal analysis of changes in fitness, physical activity, fatness and screen time. *Acta Paediatrica, 99*(1), 140-144. doi:10.1111/j.1651-2227.2009.01536.x

American Academy of Pediatrics. (2011). Media use by children younger than 2 years. *Pediatrics, 128*(5), 1040-1045. doi:10.1542/peds.2011-1753

American Academy of Pediatrics, Committee on Public Education. (1999). Media education. *Pediatrics, 104*(2), 341-343.

American Academy of Pediatrics, Committee on Public Education. (2011). Media education. *Pediatrics, 128*(5), 1-6. doi:10.1542/peds.2011-1753

Anderson, S., Economos, C., & Must, A. (2008). Active play and screen time in US children aged 4 to 11 years in relation to socio-demographic and weight status characteristics: A nationally representative cross-sectional analysis. *BMC Public Health, 8*, 366.

Bajovic, M. (2012). Violent video game playing, moral reasoning, and attitudes towards violence in adolescents: Is there a connection? (Doctoral dissertation). Retrieved from Brock University Digital Repository. (2012-10-11T15:39:11Z)

Bergh, I. H., van Stralen, M. M., Bjelland, M., Grydeland, M., Lien, N., Klepp, K. I., Anderssen, S. A., & Ommundsen, Y. (2014). Post-intervention effects on screen behaviours and mediating effect of parental regulation: The Health In Adolescents study – a multi-component school-based randomized controlled trial. *BMC Public Health, 14*(200), doi:10.1186/1471-2458-14-200

Carli, V., Hoven, C. W., Wasserman, C., Chiesa, F., Guffanti, G., Sarchiapone, M., & Wasserman, D. (2014). A newly identified group of adolescents at "invisible" risk for psychopathology and suicidal behavior: Findings from the SEYLE study. *World Psychiatry, 13*(1), 78-86.

Christakis, D. A., Gilkerson J., & Richards, J. A. (2009). Audible TV is associated with decreased adult words, infant vocalization, and conversational turns: A population based study. *Archives of Pediatric & Adolescent Medicine, 163*(6), 554-558.

Christakis, D. A., & Zimmerman, F. J. (2006). Media as a public health issue. *Archives of Pediatrics & Adolescent Medicine, 160*(4), 445-446.

Christakis, D. A., & Zimmerman, F. J. (2007). Violent television viewing during preschool is associated with antisocial behavior during school age. *Pediatrics, 120*(5), 993-999.

Christakis, D. A., Zimmerman, F. J., DiGiuseppe, D. L., & McCarthy, C. A. (2004). Early television exposure and subsequent attentional problems in children. *Pediatrics, 113*(4), 708-713.

Crespo, C. J., Smit, E., Troiano, R. P., Bartlett, S. J., Macera, C. A., & Andersen, R. E. (2001). Television watching, energy intake, and obesity in US children: Results from the third national health and nutrition examination survey, 1988–1994. *Archives of Pediatrics & Adolescent Medicine, 155*(3) 360-365.

Danielsen, Y. S., Júlíusson, P. B., Nordhus, I. H., Kleiven, M. M., Meltzer, H. M., Olsson, S. G., & Pallesen, S. S. (2011). The relationship between life-style and cardio-metabolic risk indicators in children: The importance of screen time. *Acta Paediatrica, 100*(2), 253-259. doi:10.1111/j.1651-2227.2010.02098.x

De Lacey, M. (2012, June 19). Mothers now prefer handing over smartphones rather than dummies to comfort crying babies. *Daily Mail Online*. Retrieved from http://www.dailymail.co.uk/femail/article-2161533/Mothers-prefer-smartphones-dummies-comfort-crying-babies.html

Elder, C., Gullion, C., Funk, K., DeBar, L., Lindberg, N., & Stevens, V. (2012). Impact of sleep, screen time, depression and stress on weight change in the intensive weight loss phase of the LIFE study. *International Journal of Obesity, 36*(1), 86-92. doi:10.1038/ijo.2011.60

Eron, L. D., Huesmann, L. R., Lefkowitz, M. M., & Walker, L. O. (1972). Does television cause aggression? *American Psychologist, 27*, 253-63.

Ferguson, C., & Rueda, S. M. (2010). The Hitman study: Violent video game exposure effects on aggressive behavior, hostile feelings, and depression. *European Psychologist, 15*, 99-108.

Field, A. (2009). Discovering statistics using SPSS, third edition. New York, NY: Sage.

Gentile, D. A., Reimer, R. A., Nathanson, A. I., Walsh, D. A., & Eisenmann, J. C. (2014). Protective effects of parental monitoring of children's media use: A prospective study. *JAMA Pediatrics, 168*(5), 479-484. doi:10.1001/jamapediatrics.2014.146

Goldfarb, S., Coletta, C., Moran, E., Berg, T., Schnakenberg, R. E., Gustainis, J., Kupferberg, A. (2012). 1950s: TV and Radio. In C. Johnson & L. W. Baker (Eds.), Bowling, Beatniks, and Bell-Bottoms (2nd ed., Vol. 3, pp. 797-844). Detroit: UXL. Retrieved from http://ic.galegroup.com/ic/uhic/ReferenceDetailsPage/ReferenceDetailsWindow?failOverType=&query=&prodId=UHIC&windowstate=normal&contentModules=&display-query=&mode=view&displayGroupName=Reference&limiter=&currPage=&disableHighlighting=true&displayGroups=&sortBy=&search_within_results=&p=UHIC%3AWHIC&action=e&catId=&activityType=&scanId=&documentId=GALE%7CCX1303400067&source=Bookmark&u=newh97416&jsid=3006068920e8bcaf7de36ba4dd84cf7a

Hutcheson, G. & Sofroniou, N. (1999). *The multivariate social scientist: Introductory statistics using generalized linear models*. Thousand Oaks, CA: Sage Publications.

Jago, R., Thompson, J. L., Sebire, S. J., Wood, L., Pool, L., Zahra, J., & Lawlor, D. A. (2014). Cross-sectional associations between the screen-time of parents and young children: Differences by parent and child gender and day of the week. *International Journal of Behavioral Nutrition and Physical Activity, 11*(1), 54. doi:10.1186/1479-5868-11-54

Janssen, C. (2014). Mobile application (mobile app). *Techopedia*. Retrieved August 30, 2014, from http://www.techopedia.com/definition/2953/mobile-application-mobile-app

Johnson, J., Brook, J., Cohen, P., & Kasen, S. (2007). Extensive television viewing and the development of attention and learning difficulties during adolescence. *Archives of Pediatrics & Adolescent Medicine, 161*(5), 480-486.

Kaiser, H. F. (1970) A second generation little jiffy. *Psychometrika, 35*(1), 111-117.

Mayo Clinic. (2013, August 16). Children and TV: Limiting your child's screen time. *mayoclinic.org*. Retrieved from http://www.mayoclinic.org/healthy-lifestyle/childrens-health/in-depth/children-and-tv/art-20047952

Mowder, B. A. (2005). The Parent Development Theory: Understanding parents, parenting perceptions, and parenting behaviors. *Journal of Early Childhood and Infant Psychology, 1*, 45-64.

Nielsen. (2011). U.S. parents say almost a third of the apps on their phone were downloaded by their children. *Nielsen.com*. Retrieved on August 31, 2014, from http://www.nielsen.com/us/en/insights/news/2011/u-s-parents-say-almost-a-third-of-the-apps-on-their-phone-were-downloaded-their-children.html

Nielsen. (2014). Nielsen estimates 116.3 million TV homes in the U.S., up 0.4%. *Nielsen.com*. Retrieved August 24, 2014, from http://www.nielsen.com/content/corporate/us/en/insights/news/2014/nielsen-estimates-116-3-million-tv-homes-in-the-us.html

Nunez-Smith, M., Wolf, E., Huang, H. M., Emanuel, D. J., & Gross, C. P. (2008). *Media + child and adolescent health: A systematic review*. Washington, DC: Common Sense Media.

Pagani, L., Fitzpatrick, C., Barnett, T. A., & Dubow, E. (2010). Prospective associations between early childhood television exposure and academic, psychosocial, and physical well-being by middle childhood. *Archives of Pediatrics & Adolescent Medicine, 164*(5), 425-431. doi:10.1001/archpediatrics.2010.50

Pempek, T. A., Kirkorian, H. L., & Anderson, D. R. (2010, March). The impact of background TV on the quantity and quality of parentse and academic. Paper presented at the *biannual International Conference on Infant Studies*, Baltimore, MD.

Prot, S., McDonald, K. A., Anderson, C. A., & Gentile, D. A. (2012). Video games: Good, bad, or other? *Children, Adolescents and the Media, 59*(3), 647-658. doi:10.1016/j.pcl.2012.03.016

Rideout, V. (2011). *Zero to eight: Children's media use in America*. San Francisco, CA: Commonsense Media.

Roberts, D. F., & Foehr, U. G. (2008). Trends in media use. *Children & Electronic Media, 18*(1), 11-37.

Russell, B. (1930). Are parents bad for children? Don't let Watson and Freud frighten you. It's perfectly safe to love your children if you want to. *Parents Magazine, 5*(5), 18-19.

Schmidt, M. E., Pempek, T. A., Kirkorian, H. L., Frankenfield, A. F., & Anderson, D. R. (2008). The effects of background television on the toy play behavior of very young children. *Child Development, 79*, 1137-1151.

Silver, K. (2011). Best iPhone apps for your baby, *Parents Magazine*, Retrieved March 12, 2013, from, http:// www.parents.com/fun/entertainment/gadgets/best-iphone-apps-for-baby/

Steele, M. M., Richardson, B., Daratha, K. B., & Bindler, R. C. (2012). Multiple behavioral factors related to weight status in a sample of early adolescents: Relationships of sleep, screen time, and physical activity. *Children's Health Care, 41*(4), 269-280. doi:10.1080/02739615.2012.721721

Storey, M., & French, S. (2004). Food advertising and marketing directed at children and adolescents in the US. *International Journal of Behavioral Nutrition and Physical Activity, 1, 3*. doi:10.1186/1479-5868-1-3

Van Lippevelde, W., Bere, E., Verloigne, M., van Stralen, M. M., De Bourdeaudhuij, I., Lien, N., . . . Maes, L. (2014). The role of family-related factors in the effects of the UP4FUN school-based family-focused intervention targeting screen time in 10- to 12-year-old children: The ENERGY project. *BMC Public Health, 14*, 857. doi:10.1186/1471-2458-14-857

Worthen, B. (2012, September 29). The perils of texting while parenting. *The Wall Street Journal*. Retrieved from http://www.wsj.com/articles/SB10000872396390444772404577589683644202996

Zimmerman, F. J., Christakis, D. A., & Meltzoff, A. N. (2007). Television and DVD/video viewing in children younger than 2 years. *Archives of Pediatrics & Adolescent Medicine, 161*(5), 473-479.

List of Contributors

Shagufta Asar is currently a fifth-year doctoral student in the School-Clinical Child Psychology program at Pace University-New York City. She is completing her internship at the New York Center for Child Development. Shagufta has been actively involved in research for many years and joined the Parent-Child Institute in September 2011. She participated in data collection, entry, and analysis for the Parent Behavior Importance Questionnaire-Revised (PBIQ-R) as well as the Screen Time Questionnaire (STQ). Furthermore, Shagufta has collaborated in publications and presentations for both the American Psychological Association (APA) and the National Association of School Psychologists (NASP). Her primary research interests include understanding the use of screen time as well as research related to multicultural and internationally diverse parenting activities.

Alixandra Blackman, Psy.D., is a recent graduate from Pace University's combined School-Clinical Child Psychology doctoral program. Currently, Alix has two post-doctoral fellowships in the New York area. She works part-time as a school psychologist at The School at Columbia University, a K-8 independent school affiliated with the university. In addition, she works at Nightingale Neuropsychological and Psychotherapy Services, a group private practice in Brooklyn, New York, where she conducts neuropsychological testing and provides parenting work and psychotherapy for children, adolescents, and adults. Alix's research interests include screen time and parenting, in particular, the level of distraction that screen time causes for individuals performing the parent role and the potential impact of this on the parent-child relationship.

Ashley Bogatch is a sixth-year doctoral student in the School-Clinical Child Psychology doctoral program at Pace University. She grew up on Long Island, New York, and now lives in Queens, New York. Ashley currently works at SCO Family of Services in a residential setting with adolescents and young adults who are dually diagnosed with emotional disorders and developmental disabilities. She enjoys working with this challenging yet endearing population. Ashley's primary research interests in the field of psychology include anxiety in children with food allergies, parenting, and screen time. In her spare time, Ashley likes to read, play tennis, and spend time with her loved ones.

Allison Marie Hill is a third-year doctoral student in the School-Clinical Child Psychology program at Pace University. Prior to beginning her doctoral studies, Allison worked as a professional school counselor and school-based therapist with underserved children in Nashville, Tennessee. Her interests include advancing outcomes-based mental health research in schools and using evidence-based practices to support wider program implementation. Additionally, Allison is interested in early child development, including strengthening collaboration between parents, schools, and pediatric primary care settings. Currently, Allison is a student therapist at the McShane Center for Psychological Services.

Renee Krochek, Psy.D., is a school and clinical psychologist who earned her doctoral degree at Pace University. Dr. Krochek's experiences are diverse and include working in schools with regular education and special education students and in inpatient and outpatient clinics with individuals across the lifespan. Currently a school psychologist at a private school in Brooklyn, New York, she strives to help children do well academically, behaviorally, and emotionally. She also conducts therapy and psychological assessments in private practice. To accompany her school and clinical work, Dr. Krochek's research interests and publications explore the areas of parenting and child development. She is also an adjunct faculty member at Pace University.

Barbara Mowder, Ph.D., is the director of graduate psychology programs and of the Parent-Child Institute at Pace University-New York City. She graduated with a doctorate in school psychology from Indiana University and, subsequently, has written extensively about the provision of school psychological services, infant and early childhood psychology, and parenting. In addition, she has made numerous professional presentations at, for instance, the American Psychological Association and the National Association of School Psychologists. Currently, her major areas of interest are the history of parenting, the development of parent assessment measures, and research associated with the Parent Development Theory.

Linda Escobar Olszewski, Psy.D., is a post-doctoral fellow at the Mount Sinai Adolescent Health Center (MSAHC). She graduated with a doctorate in school and clinical child psychology from Pace University, earning the award of "Outstanding Contributions to the Psychology Department." Dr. Olszewski also holds an M.A. in psychology and an M.S.Ed. in school psychology with a bilingual extension (Spanish/English). During her graduate studies, Dr. Olszewski has been active in research and has developed a keen interesting in adolescents and understanding how technology may influence both their development and mental health.

Jessica Retan is a Psy.D. candidate in her third year of Pace University's School-Clinical Child Psychology program. She holds a master's degree in psychology from The New School, where she studied attachment theory and the intergenerational transmission of trauma as part of a research team investigating the efficacy of a group attachment-based intervention (GABI). Her previous work explores parental representations and disordered eating as well as the use of screen time in the parent-child relationship. Prior to her career as a psychologist, Jessica was trained as a social worker at Hawai'i Pacific University. She believes that this training created an important foundation in understanding the psychology of children within their respective family, school, and community systems.

GENERAL ARTICLES

Evaluation of a Modified Check-in/Check-out Intervention for Young Children

Zachary LaBrot, Brad Dufrene, Keith Radley, and Jamie Pasqua

Abstract

Check-in/Check-out (CICO) has been shown to be effective for improving the behavior of students in elementary and secondary education settings. However, no studies have evaluated the relative effectiveness of CICO in early childhood settings or preschools (e.g., an Early Head Start classroom). Preschool classrooms and other early childhood environments are markedly different from elementary and secondary education settings in terms of classroom structure, behavioral expectations, and child developmental level. For these reasons, it is important to modify intervention procedures to accommodate these differences for young children. The purpose of this study was to 1) evaluate the feasibility of CICO in an early childhood setting, Early Head Start, 2) assess the social validity of CICO as rated by Early Head Start teachers, and 3) explore the effects of CICO on improving the behavior of Early Head Start children who are at risk for emotional and/or behavioral disorders. Three male children between the ages of 2 years and 5 months and 3 years and 7 months participated in this study. A changing criterion design was used to test the effects of CICO for improving teachers' ratings of the children's displays of appropriate behavior. Results indicate that the CICO intervention modified for early childhood settings was feasible, rated as socially valid by the one teacher that rated the social validity of CICO, and effective for improving the behavior of young children as rated by teachers on a Daily Behavior Report Card (DBRC).

Keywords: behavior intervention, check-in/check-out, early intervention

Evaluation of a Modified Check-in/Check-out Intervention for Young Children

Recent findings suggest that successful transition into more formal years of schooling (i.e., elementary and middle school) is often mediated by social, emotional, and behavioral skill repertoires exhibited during early childhood (Carter et al., 2010). Risk factors such as poverty, early behavioral difficulties, family discord, and parent/guardian education level often influence children's behavioral development from an early age (Carter et al.; Egger & Angold, 2006; Raver et al., 2009), resulting in substantial numbers of preschool-aged children who are at risk for developing emotional and behavioral disorders such as depression, anxiety, and conduct disorder (Carter et al.; Egger & Angold, Lavigne, LeBailly, Hopkins, Gouze, & Binns, 2009). In fact, Carter et al. reports that approximately 32% of young children entering formal schooling meet criteria for diagnosable psychiatric disorders.

Fortunately, early intervention practices have been shown to be useful for altering a child's behavioral trajectory (Raver et al., 2009; Webster-Stratton & Herman, 2010). For example, implementing a three-tiered model of prevention and intervention (Bradshaw, Mitchell, & Leaf, 2010; Fox, Carta, Strain, Dunlap, & Hemmeter, 2010) is beneficial because it allows young children to be educated in natural environments with supports that are tailored to families' unique needs (Fox et al.). The pyramid model is an example of this tiered system and includes effective strategies for prevention and early intervention for behavioral difficulties (Fox et al.; Hemmeter, Fox, Jack, & Broyles, 2007). Similarly, School Wide Positive Behavior Intervention Supports (SWPBIS) incorporates the delivery of evidence-based interventions to promote the social, emotional and behavioral development of young children while providing more intensive interventions for children who have deficits or challenges in those areas (Fox et al.; Horner, Sugai, & Anderson, 2010). Such practices exist within three tiers, with each tier consisting of more intensive, individualized interventions (Fox et al.; Horner et al.).

Tier 1 includes universal supports that promote all children's healthy social, emotional, and behavioral functioning (Fox et al., 2010; Riley-Tillman, Methe, & Weegar, 2009) through instruction for appropriate behaviors (Fox et al.; Riley-Tillman & Burns). Additionally, Tier 1 supports include the provision of nurturing, responsive, and supportive caregiving for children (Fox et. al.). Furthermore, Tier 1 includes consistent consequences for appropriate and inappropriate behaviors (Campbell & Anderson, 2011), strategies to increase child engagement (Barnett et al., 2006), the use of developmentally and culturally appropriate teaching approaches, and environments designed to promote active learning and appropriate behaviors (Fox et. al.). Successful implementation of Tier 1 supports can be effective for approximately 80-85% of children (Walker et al., 1996). However, some young children will require more targeted interventions to address social and behavioral concerns.

When primary preventative strategies are ineffective in managing behavior, Tier 2 supports can be effective for preventing undesirable outcomes for children who are considered at risk for early behavioral difficulties (Fox et al., 2010; Hawken & Johnston, 2007). Tier 2 supports involve the use of targeted interventions to reduce or eliminate children's emerging problem behaviors (Horner et al., 2010). These interventions involve identifying social-emotional skills necessary for healthy development, implementing systematic and focused instruction to teach appropriate behaviors, and developing and using data collection procedures for monitoring progress (Fox et al.). Check-in/Check-out (CICO) has emerged as a common Tier 2 intervention within SWPBIS. CICO involves clearly communicating behavioral expectations to children, coaching them to meet behavioral expectations, giving feedback at regular intervals during the day via a Daily Behavior Report Card (DBRC), and providing an opportunity to earn a reward for meeting behavioral expectations (Filter et al., 2007; Riley-Tillman, Chafouleas, & Briesch, 2007).

Each day during CICO, the child checks in with an assigned mentor (e.g., school paraprofessional) at the beginning of a school day. Check-ins typically include the mentor's review of daily expectations (e.g., follow teacher instructions) that are written on a DBRC as well as provision of specific instructions as to how to achieve these expectations (e.g., "You have to follow the teacher's directions the first time they are given"). The DBRC lists the behavioral expectations that children should follow and includes a place for teachers to evaluate the extent to which children met behavioral expectations (Hawken & Johnston, 2007). After the initial check-in, teachers evaluate the child's performance throughout the day as indicated by the times listed on the DBRC. At the end of the day, children check out with their mentor, who tallies up the DBRC scores and provides reinforcement (verbal and/or tangible) to the child for meeting his or her daily point goal (Hawken & Johnston). Finally, children bring their DBRC home for parents to sign, and parents may provide further reinforcement and/or feedback as necessary (Hawken & Johnston).

Although CICO has been found to be an effective Tier 2 intervention for students in elementary settings (e.g., Filter et al., 2007; Hawken, 2006; Hawken & Johnston, 2007; Hawken, MacLeod, & Rawlings, 2007; Hawken, O-Neill, & MacLeod, 2011), no studies have evaluated its use with young children in early childhood settings (e.g., Early Head Start). Despite the lack of empirical support for implementation in early childhood settings, individual components of CICO have been found to be useful for young children.

The CICO intervention increases antecedent pre-corrections for appropriately engaged behavior by providing frequent reminders of behavioral expectations (Filter et al., 2007), which have been shown to be an effective intervention component for young children (LeGray, Dufrene, Mercer, Olmi, & Sterling, 2013; Stormont, Smith, & Lewis, 2007). For example, LeGray et al., found that pre-teaching and differential reinforcement for appropriate behavior improved the behavioral performance of two preschool and two kindergarten children. CICO also increases adult feedback and praise, improves classroom/daycare structure, and allows for families to receive feedback about their child's behavior (Filter et al.), all of which have been shown to be effective intervention components for improving behavioral and social-emotional outcomes for young children (Dishion et al., 2008; Raver et al., 2009; Stormont et al.). Specifically, adult feedback that targets young children's display of appropriate behavior and use of social problem-solving skills (both components of CICO) are important intervention components that promote positive social and emotional development (Hemmeter, Ostrosky, & Fox, 2006).

CICO also includes school–home communication, which allows families the opportunity to engage in contingency management at home based on children's behavior during the day at school. Parental involvement with school during early childhood is linked to lower antisocial behaviors in adolescence (Dishion et al., 2008). Furthermore, the use of CICO may be beneficial for promoting a more structured and predictable environment for young children who are learning to comply with daily classroom routines (Riley-Tillman et al., 2007; Hawken & Johnston, 2007).

Although implementation of CICO with elementary students has well-defined steps (e.g., Hawken & Johnston, 2007; Miller, Dufrene, Sterling, Olmi, & Bachmayer, 2014), implementation with young children may require modifications to standard protocol as preschool and early childhood settings are substantially different in environmental structure and children's developmental levels. As such, Hawken and Johnston proposed the following modifications to CICO for early childcare settings: (a) CICO may be implemented class-wide; (b) a teacher or teacher's assistant serves as a CICO mentor instead of a non-teacher mentor; (c) DBRC utilizes developmentally appropriate visual stimuli (e.g., smiley faces that correspond with favorable ratings); (d) children check-out with their teacher; (e) children receive verbal/tangible reinforcement for meeting their DBRC goal; and (f) the teacher meets with the child to summarize intervention data. Hawken and Johnston also suggest that the teacher, teacher's assistant, and behavior specialist examine the data as opposed to a predetermined behavior team. Although Hawken and Johnston provided recommendations for implementing CICO in early childcare settings, there are currently no published studies that have tested the feasibility or effectiveness of CICO in early childcare settings.

Purpose of the Study

There is emerging empirical support for the efficacy of CICO for improving the behavioral performance of elementary students (e.g., Filter et al., 2007; Hawken et al., 2007; Hawken et al., 2011). Additionally, individual CICO components (e.g., clearly communicated behavioral expectations, differential reinforcement, school-home communication) have been shown to improve the behavioral performance of young children in early childcare settings (e.g., Dishion et al., 2008; Fox et al., 2010; LeGray et al., 2013; Stormont et al., 2007). However, there are no published reports of the feasibility or effectiveness of CICO in early childcare settings. This study was designed to (1) evaluate the feasibility of CICO in an early childhood setting, Early Head Start, (2) assess the social validity of CICO, and (3) explore the effectiveness of CICO for improving young children's behavior.

Method

Participants and Setting

Two Early Head Start teachers and three children in one Early Head Start center participated in this study. The Early Head Start center implemented SWPBIS in all classrooms. Prior to the start of the school year, all Head Start personnel attended a large group didactic training session on the implementation of SWPBIS procedures. The training focused on core Positive Behavior Intervention Supports (PBIS) components such as teacher use of behavior-specific praise, effective instruction delivery, strategies to teach and recognize appropriate behaviors, and the promotion of social and emotional development (e.g., Bradshaw et al., 2010; Everett, Olmi, Edwards, & Tingstrom, 2005). Teachers were also provided a SWPBIS manual that detailed the procedures and strategies within each tier of the tiered process (i.e., pyramid). Following the staff-wide training session, SWPBIS consultants conducted biweekly visits to the center to evaluate SWPBIS implementation, monitor program effectiveness, and provide consultation to teachers for classroom management and for individual children referred for intervention services.

All children received Tier 1 supports and were transitioned to Tiers 2 and 3 based on the severity and frequency of problem behavior and teacher referral concern. Specifically, this tiered referral process required teachers to complete and submit behavior incident reports on children's disruptive behaviors (e.g., aggression, noncompliance). If a child received four incident reports within a two-week period, had an urgent administrative concern, or a parent requested intervention services, children were transitioned to Tier 2 or 3. This center's SWPBIS plan provided CICO and/or social skills instruction as standard Tier 2 interventions. Immediately following the implementation of Tier 2 services, children's response to Tier 2 intervention was monitored via a DBRC. If data indicated a lack of response to intervention, children were then referred for Tier 3 services. Tier 3 services included functional behavior assessment and an individualized behavioral intervention plan (Bellone, Dufrene, Tingstrom, Olmi, & Barry, 2014; Dufrene, Doggett, Henington, & Watson, 2007).

The Early Head Start center included in this study served children between 4 months old and 3 years old. The Head Start agency that operated the center operated Early Head Start and Head Start centers in one rural county in a southeastern state. The child population for the agency was 73% African American, 13% Caucasian, 13% Hispanic or Asian, and 1% unspecified. As defined by Head Start entry criteria, all children were from families with income at or below the federally defined poverty line.

Child participants were referred for inclusion in the study by two teachers: Ms. Lilly (pseudonyms used throughout), an African American female with one year of experience as an Early Head Start teacher, and Ms. Robin, an African American female with an associate's degree in early child development (CDA) and one year of experience as an Early Head Start teacher. Following referral for inclusion, a behavior specialist conducted semi structured interviews with the children's teachers. During the interviews, the behavior specialist gathered information regarding participants' behavior and relevant contextual variables (i.e., antecedents, consequences), in order to develop operational definitions of behavior. Ted, a 2-year-, 5-month-old African American male, was referred to the behavior specialist for exhibiting noncompliance (i.e., failure to initiate compliance with a teacher's demand within 5 seconds of delivery) and tantrum behavior (i.e., screaming, crying, throwing toys and chairs, falling on the ground, and knocking objects over). Marshall, a 3-year-, 3-month-old African American male, was referred for noncompliance and aggression (i.e., physical contact with his hand and another person's body in a hitting, punching, pinching, pushing, or slapping motion; physical contact with his leg and another person's body in a kicking motion; physical contact with his mouth and another person's body in a biting motion; taking toys and other objects from peers without permission). Barney, a 3-year-, 7-month-old African American male, was referred for noncompliance and tantrum behavior.

All three children had previously been screened upon entry into Early Head Start with the Ages and Stages Questionnaires: Social-Emotional (ASQ:SE) Questionnaire (Squires, Bricker & Twombly, 2002). The ASQ:SE may be used with children between 36 and 66 months of age. The ASQ:SE is used to identify social or emotional developmental concerns that require further evaluation (Squires et. al., 2002). Scores obtained from the ASQ:SE are compared to established cutoff scores. A high total score is suggestive of the need for further evaluation, whereas a low total score indicates social and emotional behavior appropriate for the child's age. Based on teacher ratings, Ted, Marshall, and Barney obtained high scores (185, 105, and 90, respectively), which were well above the suggested 59-point cutoff for referral on the 36-month interval.

Intervention took place in participants' classrooms, which included approximately 3.25 square meters of usable indoor space per child that was available for the care and use of children (i.e., exclusive use of bathrooms, halls, kitchen, staff rooms, and storage places). The Early Head Start classroom contained two tables and eight chairs, a book area with a small bookshelf, and a carpet area on the opposite side of the room for teacher-led activities. At the time of the study, there were eight children (ranging from 2 to 3 years of age) and two teachers in the EHS classroom.

Measures

DBRC. Researchers collaborated with teachers to create an individualized DBRC for each child (Appendix A). Teachers and researchers identified and operationally defined desired behaviors so that they were appropriate replacements for the problem behaviors that resulted in referral for services. Each individual DBRC included two desired behaviors. Teachers rated children's display of the two desired behaviors at the ends of three time intervals each school day (i.e., 8 a.m.-10 a.m., 10 a.m.-12 p.m., and 12 p.m.-2 p.m.). The teacher rating system included providing a smiley face sticker for a behavior if the child engaged in that behavior for the majority of a specified time interval. As a result, each child could earn a total of six stickers per day (i.e., up to two stickers during each of the three time intervals). The percentage of stickers earned each day served as the dependent variable for this study, and it was calculated by dividing the total number of stickers earned by six and then multiplying by 100.

Ted, Marshall, and Barney's DBRC included following directions as a desired behavior. Following directions was operationally defined as complying with a teacher's request within 5 seconds of the request being delivered. Ted's DBRC also included appropriate transition from one activity to another, operationally defined as quietly remaining in line with hands and feet to self, as the second target behavior. Marshall and Barney's DBRCs included keeping hands and feet to oneself as the second desired behavior.

Social Validity. Teachers rated the social validity of CICO on the Behavior Intervention Rating Scale (BIRS, Elliott & Treuting, 1991). The BIRS includes 24 items with Likert-type ratings ranging from 1 (strongly disagree) to 6 (strongly agree) that assess perceptions on treatment acceptability, effectiveness, and time to effectiveness. Higher scores on the BIRS indicate high levels of teacher acceptability. Technical evaluations of the BIRS have identified three factors for the BIRS: acceptability (63% of variance), effectiveness (6% of variance), and time to effectiveness (4.3% of variance). Furthermore, a coefficient alpha yielded an alpha level of .97, suggesting high internal consistency for the scale (Elliott & Treuting, 1991).

Design and Experimental Conditions

Design. This study included a changing criterion design to test the effects of CICO on teachers' ratings of children's behavior. Changing criterion designs meet What Works Clearinghouse single-case design standards when they utilize at least three different criteria (Kratochwill et al., 2013), with two or more shifts in behavior in the expected direction being required to demonstrate a functional relationship between intervention and behavior (Ganz & Flores, 2009). Changing criterion designs are particularly useful in applied settings, as they allow for systematic evaluation of an intervention without withholding or withdrawing an intervention (Cooper, Heron, & Heward, 2007; Richards, Taylor, Ramasamy, & Richards, 1999).

Baseline. During the baseline phase, each participant's behavior was monitored by a teacher-completed DBRC. Participants were unaware of the DBRC and rewards were not provided contingent upon teacher ratings of participant behavior. When participants displayed a low, stable level of percentage of stickers earned on the DBRC, a phase change was implemented and the intervention phase began.

Intervention. CICO intervention procedures were implemented entirely by the participants' teachers, Ms. Lilly and Ms. Robin. Specifically, the CICO intervention was introduced using modified procedures as described by Hawken and Johnston (2007). Modified CICO included three primary components: (a) a morning meeting between the teacher and child in which the teacher reviewed the DBRC and the child's behavioral expectations, (b) three feedback opportunities during the school day (i.e., at 10 a.m., 12 p.m., and 2 p.m.), and (c) access to a tangible reward contingent upon meeting the daily goal. Rewards were provided from the Head Start program as part of the SWPBIS program (e.g., toy cars, bouncy balls).

Researchers trained teachers to implement CICO using Behavioral Skills Training (BST), which previous research has shown to be effective for training teachers to implement behavior interventions (Lavie & Sturmey, 2002; Sarokoff & Sturmey, 2004). BST involved providing verbal and written instructions, modeling intervention steps, allowing the teacher to rehearse, and providing praise and constructive feedback (Ward-Horner & Strumey, 2012). In regard to the current study, a researcher conducted training for each teacher during one 20-minute session. Additionally, on the following two school days in which CICO was implemented, a researcher coached the teachers in implementing CICO with the children. Each teacher implemented CICO with 100% integrity during the two days in which an experimenter was present for coaching.

Each school day when CICO was implemented, the teacher met briefly (approximately 3 minutes) with the child to review behavioral expectations on the DBRC and provide examples and counter examples of desired behaviors. Next, the teacher provided feedback to the child at 10 a.m., 12 p.m., and 2 p.m. regarding the extent to which the child had engaged in the desired behavior during the previous time interval. Teacher feedback included showing the DBRC to the child and providing a sticker for the child to place on the DBRC for each behavior that the child had successfully performed during the time period. Teachers provided stickers based on their subjective appraisal of the child's target behaviors during the rating period. Additionally, the teacher provided verbal feedback to the child. For example, if a child met expectations for a particular behavior, the teacher would indicate to the child that he had met the expectation and that he was being rewarded with a sticker for meeting the expectation (e.g., "You stood quietly in line this morning, so you get a sticker!"). However, if the child did not meet expectations for a particular behavior, then the teacher provided corrective feedback (e.g., "You did not stand quietly in line, so you will not get a sticker; please stand quietly in line next time we line up").

During the final feedback session of the day, the teacher provided feedback for each expected behavior as had been done during the two previous feedback sessions, and she also provided additional praise and a tangible reward if the child met his daily goal. However, if the child did not meet his goal, then the teacher provided corrective feedback for improved performance that would facilitate meeting the daily goal on the following school day.

Intervention integrity. Researchers evaluated teachers' treatment integrity (i.e., the degree to which teachers implemented CICO) via completed DBRCs. Researchers reviewed teachers' completion of DBRCs following each day in which CICO was implemented. Researchers reviewed each DBRC to determine if teachers had completed the DBRC in its entirety, which served as a proxy for CICO implementation. Review of the DBRCs indicated that teachers completed all DBRCs in their entirety, which provides evidence for CICO implementation.

Data analysis. Researchers visually analyzed the percentage of stickers earned on the DBRC for level, trend, and variability. Additionally, nonoverlap of all pairs (NAP, Parker & Vannest, 2009) was calculated to determine intervention effect. NAP is a nonparametric method for determining data overlap between each baseline data point and each intervention data point. Technical evaluations of NAP have found a strong correlation with R2, an established effect-size statistic. NAP scores between 0.00 and 0.65 are interpreted as small effects, scores between 0.66 and 0.92 as moderate effects, and 0.93 to 1.00 are interpreted as strong intervention effects (Parker & Vannest). Teacher's ratings on the BIRS were analyzed via descriptive statistics.

Results

Children's DBRC scores are displayed in Figure 1. During baseline, all three children's percentages of stickers earned were low and stable. In fact, only one child, Barney, earned a sticker during baseline, and he earned that sticker on the first day of baseline. When CICO was implemented, all three children displayed an immediate and substantial increase in the percentage of stickers earned. During the first criterion, Ted's percentage of stickers earned was variable across the first nine CICO days; however, the percentage of stickers earned stabilized across the final 10 days of the first criterion. Moreover, Ted met his goal of 50% of stickers earned on 14 of 19 days. Marshall's percentage of stickers earned was also variable during the first criterion; however, he met his goal of 50% of stickers earned on 10 of 13 days. Barney also displayed variable sticker earning during the first criterion, but he met his goal of 50% of stickers earned on all 10 days. When the criterion for reward was increased to four stickers (i.e., 66.67% of stickers earned), Ted's overall percentage of stickers earned increased in level relative to the preceding criterion, but was still variable. Ted met his goal for stickers earned on 11 of 15 days. For Marshall, when the goal increased to four stickers, performance remained at a similar level to the previous criterion and was similarly variable. Marshall met his goal of four stickers on nine of 11 days during the second criterion shift. For Barney, when the criterion was increased to four stickers, his performance was stable at 66.67% of stickers earned on all 10

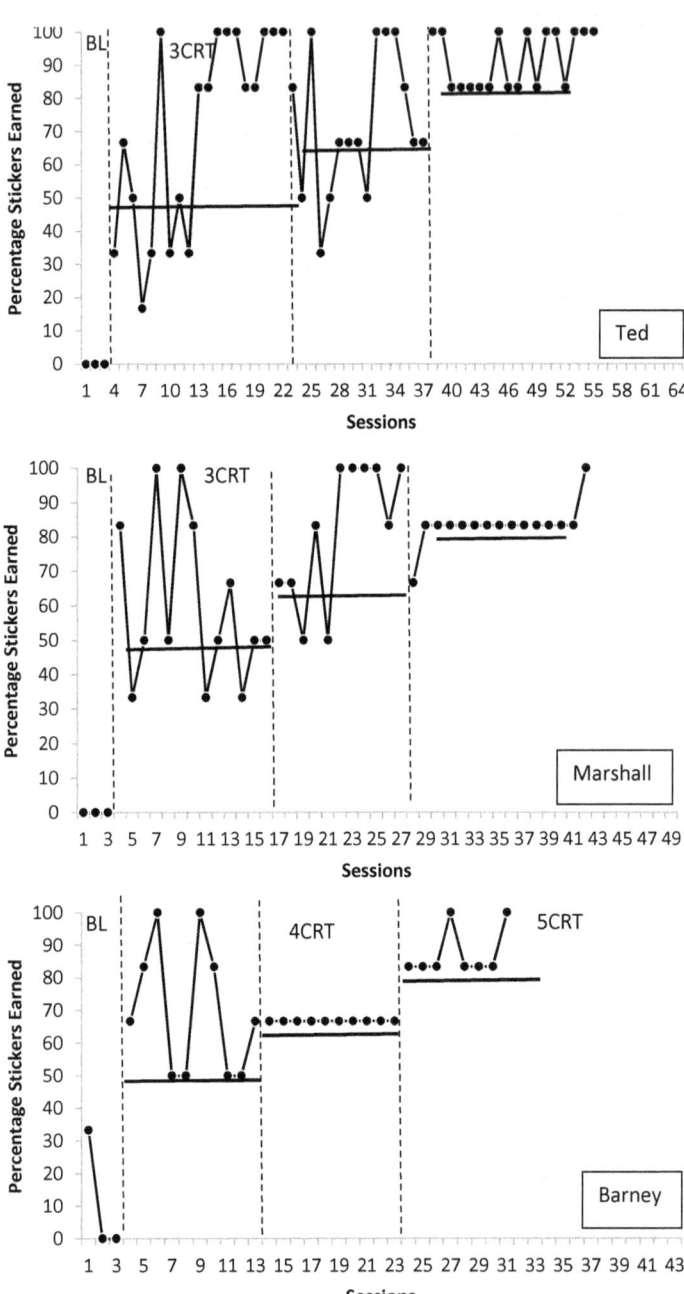

Figure 1. Percentage of Stickers Earned. BL is baseline; CRT is criterion.

days. During the final criterion shift, when the criterion for reward was five stickers (i.e., 83.33% of stickers earned), Ted's percentage of stickers earned increased in level and decreased in variability relative to the preceding criterion shift. Moreover, Ted met his goal on all 18 days. For Marshall, when the five-sticker goal was implemented, his percentage of stickers earned stabilized across all 16 sessions and he met his goal on 15 of 16 days. Finally, for Barney, when the goal increased to five stickers, his percentage of stickers earned increased in level and remained stable across eight days, and he met his goal on all eight days.

In addition to visual analysis of DBRC scores, NAP was calculated to provide an effect-size estimate for the CICO intervention. NAP was calculated by comparing baseline to CICO including all criteria shifts for each child separately. NAP scores for all children were 1.00, indicating a strong intervention effect for CICO.

Prior to the conclusion of the study, Ms. Lilly left the EHS center to work for another early childhood agency. As such, social validity data was only obtained from Ms. Robin. Ms. Robin rated the social validity of CICO and the consultation procedures with the BIRS. With regard to social validity of CICO, Ms. Robin rated every item on the BIRS a 6 (i.e., the highest possible rating), suggesting that she found CICO acceptable to use, effective for improving children's behavior, and that it improved behavior in a reasonable amount of time. Additionally, Ms. Robin indicated on the BIRS that she would use this intervention again in the future as well as recommend it to other teachers.

Discussion

This study evaluated feasibility and acceptability of a modified CICO intervention while exploring the effects on young children's behavior in Early Head Start. Although there is an emerging literature base in support of CICO for improving elementary students' behavioral performance (e.g., Filter et al., 2007; Swoszowski, McDaniel, Jolivette, & Melius, 2013), no studies have explicitly tested CICO with young children (i.e., toddlers) in early childhood settings. This study is important for at least three reasons. First, based on the integrity findings of this study, Head Start teachers implemented the modified CICO intervention with integrity as evidenced by consistently completed DBRCs and anecdotal observations of teachers conducting check-ins and check-outs made by researchers. Previous research (Miller et al., 2014; Miller, Dufrene, Olmi, Tingstrom, & Filce, 2015) indicates that elementary teachers may implement CICO with integrity, and this study extends those findings to early childhood settings.

Second, although only one teacher rated the social validity of the modified CICO intervention, that teacher rated CICO as highly socially valid. Ms. Robin's ratings for all items on the BIRS was 6 (i.e., the highest possible rating), which indicated that she found the intervention acceptable to use, effective for improving children's behavior, and that it improved behavior in a reasonable amount of time. Specifically, Ms. Robin indicated on the BIRS that she would recommend CICO to other teachers who have children exhibiting problem behavior and would use this intervention in the future due to its feasibility and effectiveness for improving child outcomes. This finding is important because it suggests that other teachers may employ these procedures because they are feasible and effective to improving young children's behavior in a timely manner. Previous research evaluating social validity of CICO has found that elementary teachers rate CICO as acceptable (e.g., Miller et al., 2014), and this study extends those findings to early childhood settings.

Finally, this study demonstrated the effectiveness of modified CICO in an early childhood setting for improving children's behavior, as evidenced by visual and statistical analysis indicating strong intervention effects. Functional relation was demonstrated between intervention implementation and behavior through three criterion changes across three children, with a mean level shift observed for each participant following an increase in criterion. Consistent with prior research, the current study demonstrates the utility of

CICO in addressing disruptive behavior (e.g., Filter et al., 2007) and provides support for utilization of the intervention with young children in early childhood settings.

Limitations and Future Research

Results of the current study must be considered in light of several limitations. First, the current study is limited by its small sample size. Future research should seek to increase the generalizability of findings through replication of procedures with a larger sample of young children. Second, this study lacked interobserver agreement data for teacher-completed DBRCs; therefore, the lack of reliability data for the DBRC may be a threat to internal validity. Third, outcome data are limited to teacher ratings of behavior on a DBRC, which are indirect measures. Fourth, it should be noted that the individuals delivering the CICO intervention (i.e., teachers) also rated children's behavior, so teachers' ratings of children's behavior may have been biased. To address both of these limitations, future research should include direct observation of children's behavior by an independent observer, as direct observation is the gold standard for behavioral assessment. However, both teachers anecdotally reported that they observed socially significant improvements in the children's behavior. In fact, Ms. Robin's ratings on the BIRS indicated that participants' behaviors improved in settings other than the classroom (e.g., recess, field trips).

Conclusion

A substantial number of young children are at risk for development of emotional and behavioral disorders (Carter et al., 2010). Successful implementation of Tier 2 interventions within a SWPBIS framework may improve behavioral trajectories of 95-99% of children (Walker et al., 1996). This study lacked a desired degree of experimental rigor related to both outcome measures and research design; therefore, the results of this study should be interpreted with caution. Despite the limitations previously noted, the current study provides preliminary support for the feasibility, social validity, and effectiveness of a modified CICO intervention for young, at-risk children. Additionally, as indicated by social validity data, these procedures are feasible and can be easily implemented by practitioners working in early childhood or preschool settings. This study is important because it is an example of the successful integration of science and practice in applied settings (Edwards, 1987). However, due to the inherent limitations in this study, future research evaluating modified CICO procedures in preschool settings is both warranted and encouraged.

References

Barnett, D. W., Elliott, N., Wolsing, L., Bunger, C. E., Haski, H., McKissick, C., & Vander Meer, C. D. (2006). Response to intervention for young children with extremely challenging behaviors: What it might look like. *School Psychology Review, 35*, 568-582.

Bellone, K. M., Dufrene, B. A., Tingstrom, D. H., Olmi, D. J., & Barry, C. (2014). Relative efficacy of behavioral interventions in preschool children attending Head Start. *Journal of Behavioral Education, 23*, 378-400.

Bradshaw, C. P., Mitchell, M. M., & Leaf, P. J. (2010). Examining the effects of schoolwide positive behavioral interventions and supports on student outcomes: Results from a randomized controlled effectiveness trial in elementary schools. *Journal of Positive Behavior Interventions, 12*, 133-148.

Campbell, A., & Anderson, C. M. (2011). Check-in/check-out: A systematic evaluation and component analysis. *Journal of Applied Behavior Analysis, 44*, 315-26.

Carter, A. S., Wagmiller, R. J., Gray, S. A. O., McCarthy, K. J., Horwitz, S. M., & Briggs-Gowan, M. J. (2010). Prevalence of DSM-IV disorder in a representative, healthy birth cohort at school entry: Sociodemographic risks and social adaptation. *Journal of the American Academy of Child and Adolescent Psychiatry, 49*, 686-98.

Cooper, J. O., Heron, T. J., & Heward, W. L. (2007). *Applied behavior analysis* (2nd ed.). Boston, MA: Pearson.

Dishion, T. J., Shaw, D., Connell, A., Gardner, F., Weaver, C., & Wilson, M. (2008). The family check-up with high-risk indigent families: Preventing problem behavior by increasing parents' positive behavior support in early childhood. *Child Development, 79*, 1395-1414.

Dufrene, B. A., Doggett, R. A., Henington, C., & Watson, T. S. (2007). Functional assessment and intervention for disruptive classroom behaviors in preschool and Head Start classrooms. *Journal of Behavioral Education, 16*, 368-388.

Edwards, R. (1987). Implementing the scientist-practitioner model: The school psychologist as data-based problem solver. *Professional School Psychology, 2*(3), 155-161.

Egger, H. L., & Angold, A. (2006). Common emotional and behavioral disorders in preschool children: Presentation, nosology, and epidemiology. *Journal of Child Psychology and Psychiatry, 47*, 313-337.

Elliott, S. N., & Treuting, M. V. B. (1991). The behavior intervention rating scale: Development and validation of a pretreatment acceptability and effectiveness measure. *Journal of School Psychology, 29*, 43-51.

Everett, G. E., Olmi, D. J., Edwards, R. P., & Tingstrom, D. H. (2005). The contributions of eye contact and contingent praise to effective instruction delivery in compliance training. *Education and Treatment of Children, 28*, 48-62.

Filter, K. J., McKenna, M. K., Benedict, E. A., Horner, R. H., Todd, A., & Watson, J. (2007). Check in/Check out: A post-hoc evaluation of an efficient, secondary-level targeted intervention for reducing problem behaviors in schools. *Education and Treatment of Children, 30*, 69-84.

Fox, L., Carta, J., Strain, P. S., Dunlap, G., & Hemmeter, M. L. (2010). Response to intervention and the pyramid model. *Infants & Young Children, 23*(1), 3-13.

Ganz, J. B., & Flores, M. M. (2009). The effectiveness of direct instruction for teaching language to children with autism spectrum disorders: Identifying materials. *Journal of Autism and Developmental Disorders, 39*, 75-83.

Hawken, L. (2006). School psychologists as leaders in the implementation of a targeted intervention: The behavior education program. *School Psychology Quarterly, 21*, 91-111.

Hawken, L., & Johnston, S. (2007). Preventing severe problem behavior in young children: The behavior education program. *Journal of Early and Intensive Behavior Intervention, 4*, 599-613.

Hawken, L. S., MacLeod, K. S., & Rawlings, L. (2007). Effects of the behavior education program (BEP) on office discipline referrals of elementary school students. *Journal of Positive Behavior Interventions, 9*, 94-101.

Hawken, L. S., O'Neill, R. E., & MacLeod, K. S. (2011). An investigation of the impact of function of problem behavior on effectiveness of the behavior education program (BEP). *Education and Treatment of Children, 34*, 551-74.

Hemmeter, M. L., Fox, L., Jack, S., & Broyles, L. (2007). A program-wide model of positive behavior support in early childhood settings. *Journal of Early Intervention, 29*(4), 337-355.

Hemmeter, M. L., Ostrosky, M., & Fox, L. (2006). Social and emotional foundations for early learning: A conceptual model for intervention. *School Psychology Review, 35*(4), 583-601.

Horner, R. H., Sugai, G., & Anderson, C. M. (2010). Examining the evidence base for school-wide positive behavior support. *Focus on Exceptional Children, 42*, 1-14.

Kratochwill, T. R., Hitchcock, J. H., Horner, R. H., Levin, J. R., Odom, S. L., Rindskpopf, D. M., & Shadish, W. R. (2013). Single-case intervention research design standards. *Remedial and Special Education, 34*, 26-38.

Lavie, T., & Sturmey, P. (2002). Training staff to conduct a paired-stimulus preference assessment. *Journal of Applied Behavior Analysis, 35*, 209-211.

Lavigne, J. V., LeBailly, S. A., Hopkins, J., Gouze, K. R., & Binns, H. J. (2009). The prevalence of ADHD, ODD, depression, and anxiety in a community sample of 4-year-olds. *Journal of Clinical Child and Adolescent Psychology, 38*, 315-328.

LeGray, M. W., Dufrene, B. A., Mercer, S., Olmi, D. J., & Sterling, H. (2013). Differential reinforcement of alternative behavior in center-based classrooms: Evaluation of pre-teaching the alternative behavior. *Journal of Behavioral Education, 22*, 85-102.

Miller, L. M., Dufrene, B. A., Olmi, D. J., Tingstrom, D., & Filce, H. (2015). Self-monitoring as a viable fading option in check-in/check-out. *Journal of School Psychology, 53*, 121-135.

Miller, L. M., Dufrene, B. A., Sterling, H. E., Olmi, D. J., & Bachmayer, E. (2014). The effects of check-in/check-out on problem behavior and academic engagement in elementary school students. *Journal of Positive Behavior Interventions*. Advance online publication. doi:10.1177/1098300713517141.

Parker, R. I., & Vannest, K. (2009). An improved effect size for single-case research: Nonoverlap of all pairs. *Behavior Therapy, 40*, 357-367.

Raver, C. C., Jones, S. M., Li-Grining, C., Zhai, F., Metzger, M. W., & Solomon, B. (2009). Targeting children's behavior problems in preschool classrooms: A cluster-randomized controlled trial. *Journal of Consulting and Clinical Psychology, 77*, 302-316.

Richards, S. B., Taylor, R. L., Ramasamy, R., & Richards, R. Y. (1999). *Single subject research: Applications in educational and clinical settings.* Belmont, CA: Wadsworth Group/Thompson Learning.

Riley-Tillman, T. C., & Burns, M. K. (2009). *Evaluating educational interventions: Single case design for measuring response to intervention.* New York, NY: Guilford.

Riley-Tillman, T. C., Chafouleas, S. M., & Briesch, A. M. (2007). A school practitioner's guide to using daily behavior report cards to monitor student behavior. *Psychology in the Schools, 44,* 77-89.

Riley-Tillman, T. C., Methe, S. A., & Weegar, K. (2009). Examining the use of direct behavior rating on formative assessment of class-wide engagement: A case study. Assessment for Effective Intervention, 34, 224-230.

Sarokoff, R. A., & Sturmey, P. (2004). The effects of behavioral skills training on staff implementation of discrete-trial teaching. *Journal of Applied Behavior Analysis, 37*(4), 535-538.

Squires, J., Bricker, D., & Twombly, E. (2002). *The ASQ:SE user's guide: For the Ages & Stages Questionnaires: Social-Emotional.* Baltimore, MD: Brookes Publishing.

Stormont, M. A., Smith, S. C., & Lewis, T. J. (2007). Teacher implementation of precorrection and praise statements in Head Start classrooms as a component of a program-wide system of positive behavior support. *Journal of Behavioral Education, 16,* 280-290.

Swoszowski, N., McDaniel, S. C., Jolivette, K., & Melius, P. (2013). The effects of Tier II Check-in/Check-out including adaptation for non-responders on the off-task behavior of elementary students in a residential setting. *Education and Treatment of Children, 36,* 63-79.

Walker, H. M., Horner, R. H., Sugai, G., Bullis, M., Sprague, J. R., Bricker, D., & Kaufman, M. J. (1996). Integrated approaches to preventing antisocial behavior patterns among school-age children and youth. *Journal of Emotional and Behavioral Disorders, 4,* 194-209.

Ward-Horner, J., & Sturmey P. (2012). Component analysis of behavior skills training in functional analysis. *Behavioral Interventions, 27,* 75-92.

Webster-Stratton, C., & Herman, K. C. (2010). Disseminating Incredible Years Series early-intervention programs: Integrating and sustaining services between school and home. *Psychology in the Schools, 47,* 36-54.

Appendix A

Child's Home-School Note

Daily Goal: _____ # out of 6 _____

I will try my best to...

	Follow Directions	Transitions (Child transitioned from one activity to another with no problems)
8:00-10:00		
10:00-12:00		
12:00-2:00		
Was the Goal Met? Yes__ No__	Reward for meeting Goal _____ _____	

_____
Teacher Signature

_____
Parent Signature

Contributors

Zachary C. LaBrot, M.A., is a 4th year doctoral student in the University of Southern Mississippi School Psychology Program and currently serves as the Mental Health Assistant for a local Head Start agency. Research interests include maintenance and generalization of skills trained through consultation as well as the evaluation of various behavioral assessments and interventions in school-based settings. Zachary and his colleagues have presented data collected through research and applied practice in early childhood settings at several regional and national conferences.

Brad A. Dufrene, Ph.D., is an Associate Professor in the Department of Psychology at The University of Southern Mississippi (USM). He is Director of the School Psychology Service Center at USM. His research interests include prevention of Emotional and Behavioral Disorders (EBD) in early childhood, especially children attending Head Start. Additionally, Dr. Dufrene is interested in testing tiered consultation procedures for increasing teachers' treatment integrity.

Keith C. Radley, Ph.D., is an assistant professor in the School Psychology Program at the University of Southern Mississippi. His research focuses on the application of behavioral interventions to address classroom behavior and social skills.

Jamie L. Pasqua, B.A., is a 3rd year graduate student in the University of Southern Mississippi School Psychology Program and serves as the P.B.I.S. Consultant for a local Head Start agency. Applied practice and research interests include early intervention services, the evaluation/ treatment of emotional and behavioral disorders, toilet training procedures, and early childhood development. Jamie and her colleagues have presented data collected through research and applied practice in early childhood settings at several regional and national conferences.

Field-validation of the COMET Mentoring Model to Enhance the Instructional Practices of Head Start Teachers

Stephen J. Bagnato, Jai Wha Seo, Jennifer Salaway, and Myoung Soon Kim

Abstract

Research Findings: The effects of a structured, individualized, and relationship-based teacher mentoring model (COMET) and its duration were examined with Head Start teachers (n = 157) in Appalachian Region III. The COMET-mentored treatment group teachers were significantly better than non-mentored teachers in applying instructional support strategies involving concept development, quality of feedback, language modeling, and classroom literacy enhancements with at-risk children. COMET teachers in the long-term mentoring group (two school years) demonstrated significantly higher competencies than those in the short-term group (one school year) in specific emotional support and instructional support strategies: teacher sensitivity, concept development, quality of feedback, language modeling, and literacy environment. *Implications for Practice, Policy, & Research*: Our results indicate clearly that the structured, individualized, and relationship-based COMET mentoring approach is superior to a traditional workshop-based approach in enhancing teachers' professional knowledge and instructional competencies; long-term COMET mentoring relationships ensured significantly better effects on the improvement of teachers' practices in instruction and classroom management than short-term mentoring. Implications for policy development on mentoring versus performance reviews; practice implementation and links to teacher evaluation; and future research on mentoring are offered.

Keywords: mentoring, intervention, professional development, classroom assessment

Introduction

Policy makers and professionals in the overarching field of early childhood intervention have tried to provide children with quality education by retaining skilled teachers (Diamond & Powell, 2011; Long, 2009). However, the field of early childhood care and education is challenged by the high attrition rate of teachers who are not motivated or not highly paid (Cummins, 2004; Howe, 2006). Teachers are often frustrated in the absence of professional support and report being overwhelmed by a sense of isolation at work, punitive performance reviews, emotional burnout, discouragement, and, often, low job satisfaction with few expectations for professional growth (Cummins, 2004; Danielson, 2002).

Importance of Teacher Mentoring

Contemporary conceptions about mentoring promote a collaborative, reciprocal, and relationship-based framework between a mentor and a mentee, while classical notions about mentoring were based on more hierarchical or subordinate relationships (Nolan, 2007). Specifically, contemporary teacher mentoring involves providing interpersonal supports based upon a collaborative and ongoing approach within a classroom setting for a less experienced practitioner to improve professional competence (Buysee & Wesley, 2009; Onchwari & Keengwe, 2010). In the field of early childhood education, mentoring has been used increasingly and advocated as an effective approach to improve teacher retention, job satisfaction, and professional enhancement (Long, 2009; Onchwari & Keengwe, 2010). The main advantage of teacher mentoring for professional development is the mentees' relatively quick acquisition of instructional competencies and knowledge under the guidance and modeling of experienced and trustworthy mentors (Diamond & Powell, 2011; Tugel, 2004). Interactive and iterative processes of observation, reflection, analysis, and experimental practices are carried out to develop teachers' competencies in supporting children's learning (Diamond & Powell; Onchwari & Keengwe). Teachers who received mentoring support acquired better competencies in planning lessons, organizing classes, managing child behaviors, and instructing language than non-mentored teachers (Diamond & Powell; Onchwari & Keengwe). Most importantly, they developed lasting professional skills and knowledge that could be used after a mentoring program was completed (Barth, 2001; Nicholls, 2002; Portner, 1998).

Another advantage of collaborative teacher mentoring is that mentees become more committed and develop higher job satisfaction through assisted socialization and reflection (Danielson, 2002; Schön, 1987). Iterative mentoring processes of reflection and feedback strengthen mentees' commitments for positive changes in their profession (Danielson; Diamond & Powell, 2011; Schön). Furthermore, mentoring creates a learning community wherein teachers benefit from emotional support and continuous stimulation for professional improvement (Danielson; Long, 2009).

Lastly, mentees' improved professional skills from the mentoring process promote children's positive development and influences their academic achievement and prerequisite social-behavioral development for school success (Evertson & Smithey, 2000; Onchwari & Keengwe, 2010). Students from mentored teachers were less distractible and showed better self-control during class, such as in paying attention and in task completion. They used more mature language and achieved higher scores in listening and speaking as well as in reading and writing. Overall, teacher mentoring has been understood as one of the most effective pathways not only for teachers' professional development, but also for children's academic and social-behavioral development (Howes, James, & Ritchie, 2003).

Snapshot of the COMET Model and Research

The current research was designed and implemented by the Center on Mentoring for Effective Teaching (COMET) at the division for Early Childhood Partnerships (www.earlychildhoodpartnerships.org) of the Office of Child Development, University of Pittsburgh, and it was funded by a federal grant from the U.S. Department of Health and Human Services, Administration on Children and Families, Office of Planning, Research and Evaluation (OPRE). The COMET initiative implemented a two-year teacher-mentoring program that included classroom observation, pretest and posttest assessments, and mentoring implementation. The COMET model consists of eight uniform and evidence-based steps (but the content is individualized for each teacher): Gaining entry and building the relationship; conducting Classroom Assessment Scoring System (CLASS) observations; setting individual CLASS goals together; selecting strategies; applying the individual mentoring plan; evaluating the plan together; holding a summary conference; planning for the future.

The design of the COMET mentoring model was based upon the objective of developing teachers' long-lasting professional competencies; this research to examine the impacts of mentoring on teachers' classroom practices was based upon five theoretical assumptions about the interrelationships among mentoring and improved instructional practices and children's early learning and school success (Diamond & Powell, 2011; Onchwari, & Keengwe, 2010; Tedder & Lawy, 2009).

First, a systematic, evidence-based mentoring process guides mentees to explore "problems in practice" and to foster the acquisition of practice competencies through a structured sequence of evidence-based steps. The COMET model consists of iterative processes of observation, pretest assessment, analysis, reflection, planning, instructional modeling, application, and monitoring (Buysee & Wesley, 2009). Goal-oriented systematic mentoring targets each mentee's specific strengths and needs on the basis of classroom observational assessment results and reflective discussion with the mentees. It provides justifications about mentors' constructive feedback and suggestions for instructional strategies and facilitates faster mentee learning with the understanding of underlying teaching principles (Buysee & Wesley, 2009; Diamond & Powell, 2011).

Second, a trained mentor provides accurate analyses of mentees' current practices, assists teachers to apply evidence-based practices, and creates a conducive learning environment in the mentees' classrooms on the basis of holistic assessment of mentees' teaching contexts (Buysee & Wesley, 2009; Danielson, 2002). On the contrary, untrained teaching staff who act as mentors tend to depend on personal experiences and beliefs rather than on accurate assessments or objective teaching principles (Evertson & Smithey, 2000), and the importance of trained mentors was emphasized for effective mentoring (Evertson & Smithey, 2000; Nolan, 2007).

Third, a collaborative mentoring relationship encourages mentees' active engagement in the change process, reduces emotional isolation at work, provides emotional supports, helps to build positive relationships with colleagues and children, and improves teaching quality in a classroom (Buysee & Wesley, 2009; Maynard & Furlong, 1993; Mullen, 2000). Accordingly, mentees' improved professional practices influence their job satisfaction, self-confidence, and motivation and commitment for work (Buysee & Wesley; Danielson, 2002).

Fourth, experienced teachers who taught five years or more, especially experienced Head Start teachers, need an "enhancement" in professional practice, because they have been working for a long time in an unchanging educational environment and their current classroom practice depends on their original education (Katz, 1972; Nolan, 2007). Although experienced teachers have long experience in teaching, the quality of their practice in the classroom is often compromised due to a lack of opportunities for updating professional competencies, isolation at work, minimum wages, and repetitive daily work without hopes of improvement (Cummins, 2004; Danielson, 2002; Nolan). Moreover, previous mentoring studies were interested in beginning teachers' professional development as a part of induction programs and excluded experienced teachers from the benefits of mentoring services (Smith & Ingersoll, 2004).

Lastly, a long-term, on-site, and regularly scheduled mentoring process helps teachers to improve professional competencies better and apply best practices consistently through internalization, because short-term mentoring may impact current practice, but it is not sufficient or effective enough to maintain positive change as teachers practice in the long term (Barth, 2001; Nicholls, 2002).

Based on the above conceptual framework, this study focused upon two research questions: 1) Do teachers, who receive individualized, on-site, on-going mentoring in the collaborative mentoring relationship demonstrate better professional practices in instruction, classroom management, and literacy development than the teachers who are not mentored? 2) Among mentored teachers, do teachers who receive a long-term, two-year mentoring intervention show better instructional and classroom management competences than those who receive relatively short-term, one-year mentoring intervention?

Method

Participants

Head Start is a national program that was established in 1965 and is funded by the U.S. Department of Health and Human Services to support low-income families and their children who are between 3 and 5 years old and are at risk for poor future academic achievement or those with developmental delays, such as in language development. Two-hundred and thirty-nine Head Start teachers, including beginning teachers with two years or less of experience in teaching (Katz, 1972) and experienced teachers—110 lead teachers and 129 assistant teachers—in low-income, rural communities in the Appalachian region of southwestern Pennsylvania and the northern panhandle of West Virginia participated in the

COMET mentoring program. Ninety-one Head Start classrooms participated and approximately 1,729 children in the classrooms were involved. A lead teacher and an assistant teacher from the same classroom were paired together as a "teaching team" and were randomly assigned to a control group or a treatment group. Depending on the participation point, teachers from a teaching team were mentored for either one year or two years by a randomly assigned mentor. On the contrary, the study did not provide any intervention to teachers in the control group until the study was completed. In this article, mentees are referred to as teachers in a treatment group.

The majority of participating teachers were female, consisting of 98% of all participants. Among them, 92% of the control group teachers and 86% of the treatment group teachers were Caucasian. Six percent of the control group teachers and 8% of the treatment group teachers were African American, and 2% of participating teachers belonged to other ethnic backgrounds. The average age for the control group teachers was 43 years old, and the average for the treatment group was 42 years old.

The average years of experience in teaching were 14 years for the control group, ranging from two to 39 years, and 11 years for the treatment group, ranging from one year to 33 years. For education level in the control group, 70% of the teachers had an associate degree or lower level of education, 19% had a bachelor's degree, and 11% had master's degrees. Similarly, in the treatment group, 62% of the teachers had associate degrees or lower; 22% had bachelor's degrees; and 16% had master's degrees.

Mentors

A total of 17 trained specialists, 14 females and 3 males, participated as mentors in this study. Participating mentors included 16 Caucasians and 1 Asian. Their average age was 36 (24 to 52 years old). Twelve mentors (71%) had either a master's degree or a Ph.D. Five were in master's degree programs or had a bachelor's degree. Mentors were university staff working at the Early Childhood Partnerships program, selected Head Start master teachers from the fields of early childhood education, or students majoring in psychology, special education, or social work.

Mentors were trained to have knowledge in child development, adult learning, subject areas of children's learning, current instruction standards, regulations of early childhood education, evidence-based classroom observation, collaborative communication, and COMET mentoring procedures and program structure. Diverse backgrounds of trained mentors provided synergic effects in the research through the sharing of their professional knowledge and experiences at monthly mentor-support meetings. Mentors were supported by program organizers and peer mentors for problem solving in the course of their mentoring practices.

The average number of hours in which a mentor engaged in mentoring intervention for a teaching team was 25.37 hours per month (5.6 hours/week). In total, 49% of mentors' intervention efforts were used to provide verbal feedback (28%), written feedback (10%), and demonstration modeling (11%). They used the rest of their efforts for analyzing mentees' current practices and planning mentoring supports such as observation of a mentee's practice (13%), resource collection (19%), goal planning (18%), and formal workshops (1%).

In addition to the mentoring role, mentors were also trained as classroom assessors with the Classroom Assessment Scoring System (CLASS; Pianta, La Paro, & Hamre, 2008) and the Early Language and Literacy Classroom Observation (ELLCO) Toolkit (Smith, Dickinson, Sangeorge, & Anastasopoulos, 2002). Those who passed reliability tests each year for the use of the CLASS assessment tool were allowed to conduct classroom assessments and mentoring. For data collection, mentors were randomly assigned to classrooms, avoiding the conflict of assessing their own mentees' classrooms during pretests and posttests.

Research Design

During the COMET preoperational stage, Head Start centers in West Virginia and Pennsylvania were established as participants in the study. Head Start teachers were invited to an orientation and were introduced to mentoring goals, benefits, responsibilities in participation, and overall processes of a mentoring intervention. In this process, COMET staff recruited teachers who volunteered to participate in the research and randomly assigned each participating teaching team to either a treatment group or a control group, respectively, using a group-randomized trial (GRT) in which clusters of "centers" were the sites for randomization (Murray, Varnell, & Blitstein, 2004). For the mentoring intervention, COMET assigned mentors randomly to a teaching team. Mentoring intervention was provided equally to a lead teacher and an assistant teacher from a teaching team in a treatment group.

A pretest was conducted before an initial mentoring intervention each year on both a control group and a treatment group, and a posttest was administered at the end of each school year to measure the effect of COMET mentoring using the CLASS (Pianta et al., 2008) and the ELLCO assessments (Smith et al., 2002). Surveys on teachers' demographics were conducted for both groups of teachers at the beginning of each school year. Mentors analyzed the CLASS assessment results to examine mentees' strengths and needs in their professional practices and initiated mentoring intervention based on their analysis and classroom observation for each teaching team for five months, from December to April, each school year. Mentors and mentees collaboratively set individualized mentoring goals and strategies in the areas of mentees' weakness or needs based on the analysis of pretest results and discussion. During a mentoring process, mentors encouraged teachers' reflection on their current professional practices and their experimentation with newly learned instructional techniques in their classrooms. As a posttest, data on teachers' classroom practices after mentoring was collected in May by randomly assigned assessors using the

CLASS and the ELLCO assessments. The process of data collection and mentoring intervention in the first year was iterated in the following year in general.

Measures

The Classroom Assessment Scoring System (CLASS) (Pianta et al, 2008) and the Early Language and Literacy Classroom Observation (ELLCO) Toolkit (Smith et al., 2002) were used to assess teachers' classroom practices at the beginning and the end of each school year as a pretest and a posttest for two school years. These measurements were chosen for their authenticity and utility in providing reliable and valid outcomes based on teachers' virtual classroom practices and were aligned with the goals of this study.

Teachers in both groups completed surveys on their background, mentoring quality, and beliefs in professional practice at the time of pretest and posttest. Likewise, mentors completed surveys on their background and mentoring quality. Additionally, they recorded their mentoring efforts each month, including mentoring strategies used, the frequency of mentoring topics used, mentoring modes, materials used, and hours spent for mentoring.

Classroom Assessment Scoring System (CLASS) Pre-K

The Classroom Assessment Scoring System (CLASS) (Pianta et al., 2008) is a research-based instrument developed for assessing teachers' competences in instruction and classroom management. It includes three domains to assess a teacher's ability to support children, including Emotional Support, Classroom Organization, and Instructional Support. Emotional Support includes four dimensions that consist of Positive Climate, Negative Climate, Teacher Sensitivity, and Regard for Student Perspectives. It measures teachers' abilities to facilitate positive relationships with children; to recognize children's needs and problems; and to promote their autonomy and leadership. Classroom Organization includes three dimensions that consist of Behavior Management, Productivity, and Instructional Learning Formats. It assesses teachers' proactive attitudes in managing children's behaviors, class preparation, and class organization for maximum learning time. Lastly, Instructional Support includes three dimensions that consist of Concept Development, Quality of Feedback, and Language Modeling. It covers teachers' competences for facilitating children's creative and analytic reasoning, providing feedback to children, and supporting language development.

The CLASS is a 7-point-scale scoring system with a *low* range of 1 and 2, a *mid* range of 3, 4, and 5, and a *high* range of 6 and 7 for each dimension except for the Negative Climate, which has a reversed 7-point scale. Dimension scores were averaged across each domain by dividing the sum of each dimension score. The CLASS has good test reliability and validity psychometrics (Pianta et al., 2008). The internal consistency is high with Cronbach's alpha .94, .89, and .89 for each domain, and the interrater reliability is also high with 87%. The four-cycle and the two-day observation stability range from .84 to .91 and .73 to .85, respectively, across dimensions. The criterion validity ranges from .33 to .63.

To maximize the reliability of each assessment, four consecutive cycles of teachers' classroom practices were observed for a pretest and a posttest, respectively. Each cycle consisted of a 20-minute observation with note taking and a 10-minute coding without interruption. Assessors chose a regularly scheduled day without special activities and tried to observe as many classroom activities as possible for an assessment. A normal school day at Head Start began at 8:30 a.m. and ended at noon. The daily schedule consisted of breakfast, transition time with hand washing for breakfast and snack, whole group circle time with book reading, small group activity with free choice play and art, outdoor play, and snack time. The CLASS is a required assessment of classroom quality and teaching practices by the federal Office of Head Start.

Early Language and Literacy Classroom Observation (ELLCO).

In addition to CLASS, the Early Language and Literacy Classroom Observation (ELLCO) Toolkit (Smith et al., 2002) was adopted to measure teachers' abilities to create literacy environments and activities. The ELLCO Toolkit consists of three tools: the Literacy Environment Checklist; Classroom Observation and Teacher Interview; and the Literacy Activities Rating Scales. Among them, this study used the Literacy Environment Checklist and the Literacy Activities Rating Scales to assess classroom layout, contents, and literacy activities such as literacy material availability; content and diversity of reading, writing, and listening materials; and literacy activities. The ELLCO has 24 items, which consist of yes or no questions and 3- or 4-point-scale scoring systems, and it takes approximately 20 minutes to complete an assessment. The measurement has high internal consistency (Brookes Publishing, 2012). The Cronbach's alpha ranges from .73 to .84 across sections, and the interrater reliability was 88%. The criterion validity, compared with Classroom Profile (Abbott-Shim & Sibley, 1998), is moderate with correlation ranging from .31 to .44 across sections.

Results

COMET Mentoring Effects on Teachers' Instructional Practices

A series of one-way, between-groups analysis of covariance (ANCOVA) was conducted to examine the difference in mentoring effects on teachers' classroom practices between the COMET treatment group and the control group and to control the effect of initial differences in teachers' instructional practices on the results of the CLASS and the ELLCO assessments. In the analysis, treatment group teachers (n = 74) who received mentoring intervention for one year and two years were compared with control group teachers (n = 83) who did not receive mentoring intervention at all in order to examine mentoring effects on teachers. In the ANCOVA analysis, the independent variable was the group with two levels, a *control group* and a *treatment group*. The dependent variables were participants' final posttest scores on the CLASS and the ELLCO assessments after the mentoring intervention was completed each school year. To control for teachers' initial differences in practice, the participants' initial pretest scores on the CLASS and the ELLCO were used as the covariates in the ANCOVA analysis.

A series of preliminary analyses of the ANCOVA assumptions, including normality, linearity, homogeneity of variances, homogeneity of regression, and the measurement of the covariate, was performed to ensure the reliability of ANCOVA analyses. The assumption of the homogeneity of regression was met for all domains and dimensions of the CLASS and for all subscores of the ELLCO Toolkit, except for the CLASS dimension of Productivity. For the analysis of Productivity, two-way mixed analysis of variance (ANOVA) was conducted with the Group as the between-subject independent variable and Time of pretest and posttest as the within-subject independent variable on the dimension of CLASS productivity.

Among the three CLASS domains, there were significant differences between the control group and the treatment group in the domain of Instructional Support and its three dimensions of Concept Development, Quality of Feedback, and Language Modeling after controlling for participants' CLASS pretest scores, $F(1, 154) = 7.819$, $p = .006$, partial $\eta^2 = .048$; $F(1, 154) = 6.514$, $p = .012$, partial $\eta^2 = .041$; $F(1, 154) = 8.909$, $p = .003$, partial $\eta^2 = .055$; $F(1, 154) = 5.279$, $p = .023$, partial $\eta^2 = .033$, respectively.

Similarly, there were significant group differences in ELLCO posttests on Book Use, Writing Around the Room, and the total scores of the Literacy Environment Checklist after controlling for the participants' pretests, $F(1, 154) = 5.902$, $p = .016$, partial $\eta^2 = .037$; $F(1, 154) = 8.400$, $p = .004$, partial $\eta^2 = .052$; $F(1, 154) = 8.884$, $p = .003$, partial $\eta^2 = .055$, respectively. Follow-up tests were performed to evaluate the pattern of differences in adjusted means on the domains and dimensions of CLASS and ELLCO subscales that produced significant differences between the control and the treatment groups. For the test, we conducted a series of post hoc pairwise comparisons, using Bonferroni correction to control for the false positive error across the comparison.

The results showed that teachers in the COMET treatment group with the mentoring intervention ($M = 2.905$, SE = .116) had significantly higher scores in the domain of Instructional Support than those in the control group ($M = 2.459$, SE = .109), after adjusting for the pretest Instructional Support score, $p = .006$ (See Table 1 for the following results of the CLASS pairwise comparison). Follow-up pairwise comparisons were conducted on the three dimensions of the Instructional Support domain to calculate the effect size for each significant pairwise comparison result. Teachers in the treatment group ($M = 2.614$, SE = .118) produced significantly higher practice scores in Concept Development than the teachers in the control group ($M = 2.200$, SE = .111) after controlling for the pretest scores, $p = .012$. In the dimension of Quality of Feedback, treatment group teachers ($M = 3.036$, $SE = .127$) were significantly better than the teachers in the control group ($M = 2.516$, SE = .120) after adjusting for the pretest scores, $p = .003$. In Language Modeling, teachers in the treatment group ($M = 3.071$, $SE = 1.128$) had significantly higher scores than the teachers in the control group ($M = 2.666$, SE = .120) after controlling for the pretest scores, $p = .023$. The effect sizes for the significant mean differences in Instructional Support, Concept Development, Quality of Feedback, and Language Modeling were in the medium range, .048, .041, .055, and .033, respectively. However, significant differences were not found in the domains of Emotional Support and Classroom Organization.

In organizing the Literacy Environment, there were significant differences between control and treatment group teachers after controlling for the ELLCO Literacy Environment pretest. Teachers in the treatment group ($M = 29.593$, $SE = .603$) had significantly better scores in the ELLCO Literacy Environment Checklist than the

Table 1:
Pairwise Comparisons and Effect Sizes of CLASS and ELLCO Posttest by Group for Treatment Effect

Group	M	Adjusted M	Adjusted mean differences (Effect Sizes in parentheses) 1	2
CLASS Instructional Support domain				
1. Control group	2.463	2.459		
2. Treatment group	2.901	2.905	.446** (.048)	
Concept Development				
1. Control group	2.193	2.200		
2. Treatment group	2.622	2.614	.414* (.041)	
Quality of Feedback				
1. Control group	2.521	2.516		
2. Treatment group	3.030	3.036	.520** (.055)	
Language Modeling				
1. Control group	2.675	2.666		
2. Treatment group	3.061	3.071	.405* (.033)	
ELLCO Book Use				
1. Control Group	4.361	4.352		
2. Treatment Group	5.216	5.227	.875* (.037)	
Writing Around the Room				
1. Control Group	6.289	6.263		
2. Treatment Group	7.338	7.367	1.104** (.052)	
Literacy Environment Checklist				
1. Control Group	27.193	27.122		
2. Treatment Group	29.514	29.593	2.471** (.055)	

Note. n = 157. *$p<.05$. **$p<.01$.
CLASS = Classroom Assessment Scoring System; ELLCO = Early Language and Literary Classroom Observation.

teachers in the control group ($M = 27.122$, $SE = .569$) after adjusting for the pretest scores, p = .003 (see Table 1 for the following ELLCO results). The effect size for the significant mean difference was .055. In Book Use and Writing Around the Room, treatment group teachers ($M = 5.227$, $SE = .262$; $M = 7.367$, $SE = .277$) showed significantly better managing skills than the teachers in the control group ($M = 4.352$, $SE = .247$; $M = 6.263$, $SE = .261$) after controlling for each of the pretest scores of Book Use and Writing Around the Room, $p = .016$ and $p = .004$, respectively. The effect sizes for the significant adjusted mean differences were .037 and .052, respectively.

Effects of COMET Mentoring Duration on Teachers' Instructional Practices

To examine group differences in the impact of mentoring duration among groups of teachers on their classroom practices, a series of one-way between subjects analysis of covariance (ANCOVA) was conducted on the outcomes of the CLASS and ELLCO assessments. The two-year mentored group (n = 44), one-year mentored group (n = 30), and non-mentored control group (n = 54) were compared by the length of teachers' mentoring intervention. In the ANCOVA analysis, the independent variable was the type of group with three levels, a control, a one-year treatment, and a two-year treatment group. The dependent variable was participants' final posttest scores on the CLASS or the ELLCO Toolkit. The participants' initial differences in the quality of classroom practice were controlled by setting each group of teachers' pretest scores as covariates.

A series of preliminary analyses of the ANCOVA assumptions, including normality, linearity, homogeneity of variances, homogeneity of regression, and the measurement of the covariate, was performed to ensure the reliability of ANCOVA analyses. The assumption of the homogeneity of regression was met for all domains and dimensions of CLASS and for all subscores of the ELLCO Toolkit, except for the CLASS dimension of Teacher Sensitivity. For the analysis on Teacher Sensitivity, a two-way mixed analysis of variance (ANOVA) was performed with the group as a between-subject independent variable and the time of pretest and posttest as a within-subject independent variable on the posttest of the CLASS in regard to Teacher Sensitivity.

Significant group differences were found on posttest outcomes among the control, one-year treatment, and two-year treatment groups in the domains of Emotional Support and Instructional Support after controlling for the participants' CLASS pretest scores, $F(2, 124) = 4.834$, $p = .010$, partial $\eta^2 = .072$; $F(2, 124) = 4.996$, $p = .008$, partial $\eta^2 = .075$, respectively. Further analyses were conducted on the dimensions of the CLASS domain with significant group differences. With the adjustment of the CLASS pretest scores, a series of ANCOVA and mixed-ANOVA analysis results showed significant group differences in Teacher Sensitivity, Regard for Student Perspectives, and in Concept Development, Quality of Feedback, and Language Modeling of the Instructional Support domain, $F(2, 125) = 3.353$, $p = .038$, partial $\eta^2 = .051$; $F(2, 124) = 4.519$, $p = .013$, partial $\eta^2 = .068$; $F(2, 124) = 4.065$, $p = .020$, partial $\eta^2 = .062$; $F(2, 124) = 4.168$, $p = .018$, partial $\eta^2 = .063$; $F(2, 124) = 5.244$, $p = .007$, partial $\eta^2 = .078$, respectively. In the ELLCO analysis, there were significant differences on posttests among group types in Book Area, Writing Around the Room, and the total score of the Literacy Environment Checklist after controlling for participants' pretest scores, $F(1, 124) = 10.641$, $p = .000$, partial $\eta^2 = .146$; $F(1, 124) = 4.779$, $p = .010$, partial $\eta^2 = .072$; $F(1, 124) = 4.722$, $p = .011$, partial $\eta^2 = .071$, respectively.

For the follow-up analyses to evaluate the pattern of differences in adjusted means, post hoc pairwise comparisons were conducted using Bonferroni adjustment to control for the false positive outcome across comparisons. To calculate the effect size of the significant group differences, a series of custom pairwise comparisons was carried out using ANCOVA and mixed-ANOVA tests. The result of the CLASS analysis showed that teachers in the two-year treatment group ($M = 5.761$, $SE = .105$) had significantly higher scores in the domain of Emotional Support than the teachers' scores in the one-year treatment group ($M = 5.261$, $SE = .128$) after adjusting for the pretest scores, $p = .009$, partial $\eta^2 = .069$ (see Table 2 for the following CLASS results of pairwise comparisons). The score of the two-year treatment group teachers was better than that of the control group teachers ($M = 5.652$, $SE = .095$) after adjusting for the pretest scores, although the group difference was not statistically significant, p = 1.000. Unexpectedly, the control group teachers had significantly better adjusted mean scores than the one-year treatment group teachers in the domain of Emotional Support, $p = .048$, partial $\eta^2 = .46$.

Further analyses were conducted on the dimensions of Emotional Support to investigate the pattern of differences and their effect sizes. In the mixed ANOVA analyses of Teacher Sensitivity, the two-year treatment group ($M = 5.119$, $SE = .103$) performed significantly better than the one-year treatment group ($M = 4.763$, $SE = .125$), $p = .029$, partial $\eta^2 = .037$. Unexpectedly, the control group was significantly better than the one-year treatment group in Teacher Sensitivity, $p = .016$, $\eta^2 = .045$. In Regard for Student Perspectives, there were significant group differences. The post hoc pairwise comparison presented that teachers in the two-year treatment group ($M = 5.228$, $SE = .143$) had significantly better scores than the teachers in the control group ($M = 4.834$, $SE = .193$) and the one-year treatment group ($M = 4.574$, $SE = .174$) after controlling for the pretest scores of the Regard for Student Perspective, $p = .043$, partial $\eta^2 = .033$; $p = .013$, partial $\eta^2 = .062$, respectively.

In the CLASS domain of Instructional Support, two-year treatment teachers ($M = 3.17$, $SE = .155$) were significantly better than the teachers from the one-year treatment group ($M = 2.535$, $SE = .187$) and the control group ($M = 2.556$, $SE = .139$) after adjusting for the pretest, $p = .037$, partial $\eta^2 = .051$; $p = .014$, partial $\eta^2 = .057$, respectively. As expected, scores of the two-year treatment group were significantly better than those of the one-year treatment group and the control group in all three dimensions of Instructional Support. In Concept Development, the teachers in the two-year treatment group ($M = 2.834$, $SE = .156$) had a significantly better score than the teachers in the control group ($M = 2.273$, $SE = .141$) and the one-year treatment group teachers ($M = 2.304$, $SE = .191$) after controlling for the pretest scores, $p = .035$, partial $\eta^2 = .055$; $p = .025$, partial $\eta^2 = .035$. In Quality of Feedback, the two-year treatment group ($M = 3.271$, $SE = .174$) showed the highest posttest scores among groups and had significant mean differences from the control group ($M = 2.620$, $SE = .156$) and the one-year treatment group ($M = 2.704$, $SE = .209$) after controlling for the pretest scores, $p = .041$, partial $\eta^2 = .033$; $p = .019$, partial $\eta^2 = .058$. The two-year treatment group teachers ($M = 3.373$, $SE = .167$) showed the highest posttest scores in Language Modeling among the three groups. They were significantly better than the control group ($M = 2.784$, $SE = .150$) and the one-year treatment group ($M = 2.609$, $SE = .200$) after controlling for the pretest scores, $p = .031$, partial $\eta^2 = .052$; $p = .012$, partial $\eta^2 = .065$.

Similarly, the follow-up post hoc pairwise comparisons of ELLCO scores showed that the two-year treatment group was significantly better than the one-year treatment group or the control group in the total scores of Literacy Environment and the subscores of Book Area and Writing Around the Room. In the ELLCO Literacy Environment Checklist, teachers in the two-year treatment group ($M = 30.554$, $SE = .803$) had significantly better scores than the teachers in the control group ($M = 27.280$, $SE = .722$) after adjusting for the pretest scores, $p = .003$, partial $\eta^2 = .069$ (see Table 2 for the following ELLCO pairwise comparison results). Furthermore, the two-year treatment group had higher scores than the one-year treatment group ($M = 28.150$, $SE = .971$), although the group difference was not statistically significant. The one-year treatment group teachers also had better scores than the control group teachers after adjusting for the pretest scores even though the group difference was minimal with mean difference of .871 and standard error of 1.209.

Table 2:
Pairwise Comparisons and Effect Sizes of CLASS and ELLCO Posttest by Group for Duration Effect

Group	M	Adjusted M	Adjusted mean differences (Effect Sizes in parentheses)		
			1	2	3
CLASS Emotional Support Domain					
1. Control group	5.654	5.652			
2. 1-year treatment	5.258	5.261	-.391* (.046)		
3. 12-year treatment	5.761	5.761	.109	.500** (.069)	
Instructional Support domain					
1. Control group	2.562	2.556			
2. 1-year treatment	2.547	2.535	-.021		
3. 2-year treatment	3.142	3.157	.601** (.057)	.622* (.051)	
Teacher Sensitivity					
1. Control group	5.269	5.141			
2. 1-year treatment	4.692	4.763	-.379* (.045)		
3. 2-year treatment	5.319	5.119	-.022	.357* (.037)	
Regard for Student Perspectives					
1. Control group	4.829	4.834			
2. 1-year treatment	4.583	4.574	-.260		
3. 2-year treatment	5.227	5.228	.394* (.033)	.654** (.063)	
Concept Development					
1. Control group	2.269	2.273			
2. 1-year treatment	2.325	2.304	.031		
3. 2-year treatment	2.824	2.834	.561** (.055)	.530* (.035)	

Table 2 (continued):

Group	M	Adjusted M	Adjusted mean differences (Effect Sizes in parentheses)		
			1	2	3
Quality of Feedback					
1. Control group	2.634	2.620			
2. 1-year treatment	2.733	2.704	.084		
3. 2-year treatment	3.233	3.271	.651** (.058)	.567* (.033)	
Language Modeling					
1. Control group	2.782	2.784			
2. 1-year treatment	2.608	2.609	-.172		
3. 2-year treatment	3.369	3.373	.591** (.052)	.763** (.065)	
ELLCO Book Area					
1. Control group	2.963	2.952			
2. 1-year treatment	2.567	2.579	-.373*** (.116)		
3. 2-year treatment	2.977	2.983	.031	.404*** (.127)	
Writing Around the Room					
1. Control group	6.167	6,177			
2. 1-year treatment	6.933	6.756	.580		
3. 2-year treatment	7.614	7.722	1.545** (.071)		.965
Literacy Environment Checklist					
1. Control group	27.370	27.280			
2. 1-year treatment	28.533	28.150	.871		
3. 2-year treatment	30.182	30.554	3.275**(.069)		2.404

Note. n = 128. *p<.05. **p<.01. ***p<.001. CLASS = Classroom Assessment Scoring System; ELLCO = Early Language and Literary Classroom Observation.

After controlling for the pretest of Book Area, the two-year treatment group teachers ($M = 2.983$, $SE = .061$) had a significantly better score than the one-year treatment group teachers ($M = 2.579$, $SE = .074$) with the mean difference of .404, $SE = .095$, $p = .000$. The effect size for this adjusted group mean difference in Book Area was large, with .127. Unexpectedly, the control group was significantly better than the one-year treatment group with the mean difference of .373 and standard error of .093, $p = .000$, partial $\eta^2 = .116$. Likewise, in the follow-up pairwise comparison on Writing Around the Room, the two-year treatment group ($M = 7.722$, $SE = .372$) was significantly better than the control group ($M = 6.177$, $SE = .335$) after adjusting for the pretest, $p = .008$, partial $\eta^2 = .071$. Furthermore, the posttest score of the two-year treatment group teachers was moderately better than those of the one-year treatment group ($M = 6.756$, $SE = .452$) with the mean difference of .965 and the standard error of .588. The one-year treatment group had better adjusted mean scores than the control group, and the mean difference was .580 with the standard error of .563, although the difference was minor.

Discussion

Results of the study supported our conceptual framework that a long-term, systematic, individualized, and on-site mentoring process within a collaborative relationship by a trained mentor promoted the development of teachers' professional competencies in instruction and classroom management (Evertson & Smithey, 2000; Howes et al., 2003; Tedder & Lawy, 2009). In addition, the study results addressed four important elements, which are meaningful and distinguish this research from previous studies.

First, the study demonstrated that mentoring intervention is effective not only for beginning teachers but also for experienced teachers' professional development. Nolan (2007) and Katz (1972) asserted that teachers with five or more years in teaching, especially Head Start teachers, tend to feel stale and repetitive and need innovation in teaching. Compared to certified teachers with teaching credentials and college degrees, Head Start teachers had been working with minimum education in a difficult educational environment, in classrooms that included unmotivated children with various developmental difficulties (Cummins, 2004; Howe, 2006). These teachers often feel isolated at work with few opportunities for professional development or increased pay and are in great need for the enhancement of professional competences and commitment for work through the opportunities of teacher mentoring (Nolan).

Like most Head Start teachers, those in the study had minimum education with the Child Development Associate (CDA) certificate, which requires completion of six courses in early childhood education or related topics without college degrees or teaching credentials. Sixty-two percent of treatment group teacher had a high school diploma or an associate degree with CDA. The majority of mentees in the treatment group had been working part-time for more than five years with minimum payment and few opportunities for professional development and promotion. In spite of the field's preconception that mentoring is for beginning teachers' induction to the program by experienced teaching staff, the teachers in the study were highly interested in the opportunity for mentoring intervention to improve their professional competence. On the pretest before mentoring intervention, the treatment group teachers scored much lower than the control group teachers in eight CLASS dimensions and in all of the sections of the Literacy Environment Checklist. After mentoring, however, the treatment group teachers achieved much higher scores than the pretests in eight CLASS dimensions, and they produced significantly higher scores after mentoring intervention in all dimensions of Instructional Support posttest ($M = 2.901$, $SE = .041$) compared to the pretest ($M = 2.534$, $SE = .876$). On the contrary, the control group scored lower or saw minimal increases in the CLASS dimensions, and the posttest score ($M = 2.594$, $SE = .832$) in the same domain was decreased noticeably compared to the pretest ($M = 2.463$, $SE = .961$). Sixty-six percent of the treatment group teachers reported satisfaction with their mentoring experiences.

The study results with Head Start teachers are expected to be replicated in studies with teachers at more traditional types of preschools because those teachers have better educational levels in early childhood education and are expected to have higher sensitivity in response to a systematic evidence-based mentoring intervention than the Head Start teachers did, although the change rate may or may not be as high as the others' because their initial practice scores may be much higher than the Head Start teachers' scores.

Secondly, the evidence-based individual mentoring process proved to be critical for mentors helping mentees to focus on specific issues in need of improvement and to maximize mentoring time and efforts for professional development (Buysee & Wesley, 2009). The survey data from "How my mentor helped me" indicated that 79.5% of mentors' efforts was used for individually targeted mentoring activities and issues. In the survey, a teacher reported that her mentoring process had been satisfactory because it was an analytic and expectable process based on assessment results and individualized reflection with her mentor.

Thirdly, a trained mentor who was equipped with a wide range of knowledge in early childhood, professional development, leadership, classroom observation, and assessment proved to be highly effective in identifying and targeting mentees' professional goals based on the analysis of mentees' practices. On the contrary, mentoring by teaching staff tended to depend on personal experiences, and their mentoring effects could have been compromised in quality and outcome as well as in mentees' indication of satisfaction from mentoring experiences (Evertson & Smithey, 2000). The study results based on the mentor survey "How I helped my mentees" indicated that the mentoring quality by a trained mentor was highly related to treatment group teachers' higher proficiency in stimulating children's thought processes, utilizing feedback loops, modeling advanced language, providing topic-related books, and creating writing environments in classrooms, compared to the control group teachers. This result is supported by previous studies, which emphasized the importance of trained mentors (Buysee & Wesley, 2009; Megginson, 2000; Nolan, 2007).

To apply the mentoring model with a trained mentor in other childcare centers or preschools, we suggest that directors train their program managers as professional mentors as an option for adopting a professional mentor. Mentoring by program managers is expected to be a good option from the perspective of utilizing existing human resources and minimizing mentoring costs. However, when program managers do assume the mentor's role in childcare centers, it is critical for them to recognize the importance of maintaining supportive mentor and mentee relationships so that mentees feel comfortable and do not fear being supervised or evaluated by their bosses.

Lastly, the long-term mentoring data showed the significance of mentoring duration. The two-year, long-term treatment group produced significantly higher scores than the one-year, short-term treatment group did in all seven dimensions of Emotional Support and Instructional Support as well the Literacy Environment Checklist. This indicates that teachers' professional competency develops over a longer period of time rather than in a short period; we have observed this duration effect from other mentoring studies currently in progress. This implies that a mentoring intervention for professional development must allow sufficient time for teachers to apply and learn new teaching skills and internalize them gradually for classroom application. In other words, when mentoring intervention is terminated shortly before internalization happens, mentees may show temporary change, but their mentoring effects may fade as time goes by. Therefore, the data suggests that a long-term mentoring intervention should be planned with the consideration of maturation time in teachers' skill development and the time required for comfortable application in classrooms in the long term (Buysee & Wesley, 2009; Nolan, 2007).

Interestingly, COMET mentoring produced its most significant improvement in the domain of Instructional Support, which has been the lowest scoring and the most challenging skill area in teachers' professional competences in general (Pianta et al., 2008). Before mentoring intervention, the initial pretest score for the two-year treatment group ($M = 2.388$, $SE = .812$) was lowest among the three groups. After intervention, however, the two-year mentored group ($M = 3.142$, $SE = 1.166$) scored highest among them, and the domain score was significantly higher than the one-year treatment group ($M = 2.547$, $SE = .705$) or the control group posttest scores ($M = 2.562$, $SE = 1.032$). This result suggests that the mentoring was highly effective from the perspective that mentors accurately identified indicators and behavioral markers of Instructional Support dimensions as mentees' weakest competence areas and narrowed down accurately on the indicators and behavioral markers to target and produce positive outcomes in the dimensions. The significant outcomes in the targeted dimensions were found to be the result of the most targeted treatment effect. In addition, this significant result proved that the mentored teachers were applying newly developed instructional strategies consistently in their classroom practices at the final stage of posttest data collection (Buysee & Wesley, 2009; Onchwari & Keengwe, 2010; Weaver, 2004).

In the two-group analysis, there were no significant group differences in the dimensions of Emotional Support and Classroom Organization. In the three-group analysis, there was no significant difference in the domain of Classroom Organization. The explanations for these insignificant differences are first as a result of goal-oriented intervention and efforts in the Instructional Support dimension; the lowest dimensions' scores were significantly improved. On the contrary, mentors and mentees focused their efforts less on the other dimensions, and their scores in Classroom Organization might have showed less significant differences than the targeted dimensions.

One thing that is important that we should not misunderstand or overlook in the group comparison result is that "not significant" in the ANCOVA results does not mean that there was no increase or effect in those dimension scores from pretests to posttests. In fact, all the individual CLASS dimension scores and all the ELLCO section scores were increased at the posttest, although the increase was not statistically significant.

Across the analyses of the CLASS and the ELLCO assessments, change differences among the control, the one-year treatment, and the two-year treatment groups were more significant and extensive than those between the control and the mentored group analysis. When the data was analyzed by the duration of mentoring treatment, the two-year treatment group showed the highest professional competences in more dimensions of classroom practices and in more subscales of classroom literacy performance among the three groups. This result stood out in the three-group analysis, because the treatment effect was diluted when the one-year and the two-year treatment effects were integrated for comparison as a group with the control group without the consideration of duration in mentoring.

This result implies that, first, establishing collaborative and trustful mentoring relationships between teachers and mentors takes considerable time before they bring out positive mentoring effects in professional practices (Buysee & Wesley, 2009). Second, the modification or change in teachers' practices was more resistant in the one-year treatment group than in the two-year treatment group. The reason that the treatment effect was lower in the context of the control and the treatment group analysis is because the one-year treatment group diluted mentoring effects in the analysis. Another reason that the mentoring effects took longer to show in classroom instruction can be explained by the fact that most participants in the study were veteran teachers with an average teaching experience of 14 years for the control group and 11 years for the treatment group. As a result, the more experienced teachers in the study might have been more resistant to change than beginning teachers due to their conformity to established or habituated practice styles that they have been using for a long time. Lastly, in the beginning of mentoring intervention, experienced teachers, who generally were in a position of providing mentoring to beginning teachers rather than receiving mentoring intervention (Evertson & Smithey, 2000; Howes et al., 2003), might have experienced emotional conflict about being mentored by an outside research person and could have been more resistant to taking a mentor's suggestions in instruction.

Unexpectedly, teachers in the one-year treatment group had lower scores than teachers in the control group in some CLASS dimensions of Emotional Support and Classroom Organization. One of the explanations for this result is that the short-term relationship between a mentor and mentee impacted the mentoring outcomes significantly in the first year. As a result, the one-year treatment group might not have been as effective as the control or the two-year treatment group, considering the significant mentoring effects showed in the long term in the two-year treatment group. Establishing trustful and collaborative relationships with mentees requires lots of effort, and the rapport between a mentor and a mentee impacts mentoring outcomes (Buysee & Wesley, 2009). Another explanation for the one-year treatment group's lower scores is the John Henry effect (Cook & Campbell, 1979), which is an experimental bias from a control group who tries to overcome the disadvantage of being in a control group and therefore tries hard to exceed the outcomes of a treatment group in comparison. The control group teachers had volunteered for this mentoring research with the expectation that they would receive mentoring services, seeking an opportunity for professional development. However, they were assigned to a control group for two years, and in the absence of benefits from getting mentoring intervention they were well aware that their scores would later be compared to those of the teachers in the treatment group.

As a result, these control group teachers might have competed to exceed the treatment group teachers as a reaction to being in the control group for a long time and for being excluded from the benefits of mentoring services.

Through the COMET mentoring research, this study found teacher commitment is a critical element for the improvement of professional competence and classroom quality. Teachers' commitment is often assumed and disregarded to be developed in subordination to other professional skill development, and it is missed from being treated directly in teacher mentoring as most previous mentoring studies have focused on teaching instructional techniques for professional development (Franke & Dahlgren, 1996). When teachers' commitment is low, they are often less responsive to mentoring intervention and their learning process is delayed accordingly, leaving teachers emotionally flat in a classroom (Nolan). In addition, teachers with low motivation or commitment are inactive and tend not to try their best in class, even in the areas in which they are proficient (Buysee & Wesley, 2009; Nolan). Therefore, we highly suggest intervention treatment focusing directly on the indicators related to inspiring teachers' motivation and commitment.

Implications for Future Policy, Practice, and Research

The field-validation research for the COMET mentoring model offers a clear statement that an individualized, systematic, relationship-based, and classroom-based mentoring approach with teachers using a uniform and structured step-by-step format aligned with goals/content that are linked to "best practice" standards is highly effective in improving teaching practices. Based upon our analysis of the extant research literature in early childhood education, this study concludes that the detailed aspects of the nature, attributes, and content of individualized mentoring have not been studied as perhaps the best vehicle for improving teacher practices. While consultation approaches have been studied, individualized mentoring and features specific to its model have not been fully examined. Our current study establishes clearly that individualized mentoring improves teachers' instructional and management practices. Based upon current research outcomes, we offer several implications for changes in policy, professional practices, and future research to establish mentoring as the preferred approach both for improving teachers' practices and promoting their continuing professional development—not only in Head Start, but in all types of early childhood education and intervention programs.

Policy

The following policy implications were derived from our COMET research: 1) Mentoring is measurably more effective than the current combination of generalized professional development approaches based on annual workshops and/or annual performance reviews and 2) The Office of Head Start (OHS) within the U.S. Department of Health and Human Services must seriously consider revising their policies on Annual Performance Reviews (APRs). The APRs are viewed by teachers as negative and sometimes punitive experiences, which focus more on sanctions for their shortcomings than on promoting their professional development. In contrast, the COMET process places a premium on confidentiality, trust-worthiness, and supportive relationships using an adult-learning model of collaborative goal-setting and strategy-setting linked to the best practice standards and promoting the professionalism of the teaching teams. Teachers demonstrated great satisfaction with this supportive process and made observable improvements in teaching behaviors. Over 80% of the teachers elected to continue in the COMET model and process because of these aspects. 3) Alignment with clear and evidence-based standards of practice is a central dimension of improving teacher effectiveness. Our COMET research demonstrates clearly that collaborative goal-setting within individualized Mentoring for Effective Teaching (MET) plans based on goal-indicators derived from each teacher's pre-mentoring CLASS profile were perhaps the most effective operational feature associated with teacher improvements in instruction, emotional support for child relationships, and practices; research shows that this results in children's acquisition of early literacy skills and social and self-control behaviors. When teachers are shown the results of their CLASS profiles within a supportive relationship with a trusted mentor, their commitment to both goal-setting and change is fostered.

Professional Practices

The following implications about "best practices" were derived from our COMET research. Eight dimensions seem to be the most important "operational" elements for implementing an effective mentoring process that will improve teaching practices: mentor-mentee interpersonal relationship; a uniform, step-by-step mentoring model with training of mentors; use of the CLASS measure for observation and goal-setting; collaborative goal-setting linked to the CLASS indicators; an individualized mentoring plan of CLASS goals and mentoring strategies; evidence-based regular feedback; duration of mentoring; and quality checks based on measures of mentor and mentee perceptions. The COMET model effectively blends these eight elements into a seamless process of mentoring.

Research

The following implications for future research derive from our COMET field-validation: 1) More research is needed on the specific interpersonal qualities that equate with selecting and matching the most effective mentors to mentees and 2) Future research should focus upon the use of the CLASS assessment in numerous types of early childhood intervention settings linked to a mentoring process and how this combination of elements effectively promotes teacher effectiveness. 3) Research is needed on the cost-effectiveness and impact of "virtual" professional development and mentoring models blended with on-site mentoring within programs by program managers as mentors.

References

Abbott-Shim, M., & Sibley, A. (1998). *Assessment profile for early childhood programs*. Atlanta, GA: Quality Assist.

Barth, R. S. (2001). Teacher leader. *Phi Delta Kappan, 82*(6), 443-449.

Brookes Publishing. (2012). *ELLCO Pre-K technical appendix*. Retrieved from http://archive.brookespublishing.com/documents/ellco-pre-k-technical.pdf

Buysee, V., & Wesley, P. W. (2009). *Consultation in early childhood settings* (3rd ed.). Baltimore, MD: Brookes Publishing.

Cook, T. D., & Campbell, D. T. (1979). *Quasi-Experimentation: Design and analysis issues for field settings*. Boston, MA: Houghton Mifflin.

Cummins, L. (2004). The pot of gold at the end of the rainbow: Mentoring in early childhood education. *Childhood Education, 80*(5), 254-257.

Danielson, L. (2002). Developing and retaining quality classroom teachers through mentoring. *The Clearing House, 75*(4), 183-185.

Diamond, K. E., & Powell, D. R. (2011). An iterative approach to the development of a professional development intervention for Head Start teachers. *Journal of Early Intervention, 33*(1), 75-93.

Evertson, C. M., & Smithey, M. W. (2000). Mentoring effects on protégés' classroom practice: An experimental field study. *The Journal of Educational Research, 93*(5), 294-304.

Franke, A., & Dahlgren, L. O. (1996). Conceptions of mentoring: An empirical study of conceptions of mentoring during the school-based teacher education. *Teaching and Teacher Education, 12*(6), 627-641.

Howe, E. (2006). Exemplary teacher induction: An international review. *Educational Philosophy and Theory, 38*(3), 287-297.

Howes, C., James, J., & Ritchie, S. (2003). Pathways to effective teaching. *Early Childhood Research Quarterly, 18*, 104-120.

Katz, L. G. (1972). Developmental stages of preschool teachers. *Elementary School Journal, 73*(1), 50-54.

Long, J. (2009). Assisting beginning teachers and school communities to grow through extended and collaborative mentoring experiences. *Mentoring & Tutoring: Partnership in Learning, 17*(4), 317-327.

Maynard, T., & Furlong, J. (1993). Learning to teach and models of mentoring. In D. McIntyre, H. Hagger, & M. Wilkin (Eds.), *Mentoring: Perspectives on school-based teacher education* (pp.69-85). London, United Kingdom: Kogan Page.

Megginson, D. (2000). Current issues in mentoring. *Career Development International, 5*(4-5), 256-260.

Mullen, C. A. (2000). Constructing co-mentoring partnerships: Walkways we must travel. *Theory Into Practice, 39*(1), 4-11.

Murray, D. M., Varnell, S. P., & Blitstein, M. S. (2004). Design and analysis group-randomized trials (GRT): A review of recent methodological developments. *American Journal of Public Health, 94*(3), 423-432.

Nicholls, G. (2002). Mentoring: The art of teaching and learning. In P. Jarvis (Ed.), *The theory and practice of teaching* (1st ed., pp. 132-142). London, United Kingdom: Kogan Page.

Nolan, M. E. (2007). *Mentor coaching and leadership in early care and education.* Clifton Park, NY: Thomson Delmar Learning.

Onchwari, G., & Keengwe, J. (2010). Teacher mentoring and early literacy learning: A case study of a mentor-coach initiative. *Early Childhood Education Journal, 37,* 311-317.

Pianta, R. C., La Paro, K. M., & Hamre, B. K. (2008). *Classroom assessment scoring system: Pre-K.* Baltimore, MD: Brookes Publishing.

Portner, H. (1998). *Mentoring new teachers.* Thousand Oaks, CA: Corwin Press.

Schön, D. S. (1987). *Educating the reflective practitioner.* San Francisco, CA: Jossey Bass.

Smith, M. W., Dickinson, D. K., Sangeorge, A., & Anastasopoulos, L. (2002). *Early language and literacy classroom observation.* Baltimore, MD, MA: Brookes Publishing.

Smith, T., & Ingersoll, R. (2004). What are the effects of induction and mentoring on beginning teacher turnover? *American Educational Research Journal, 41*(3), 681-715.

Tedder, M., & Lawy, R. (2009). The pursuit of 'excellence': Mentoring in further education initial teacher training in England. *Journal of Vocational Education and Training, 61*(4), 413-429.

Tugel, J. (2004). Teacher quality: What the No Child Left Behind Act means for teacher quality and professional development. *Science and Children, 41*(5), 22-25.

Weaver, P. E. (2004). The culture of teaching and mentoring for compliance. *Childhood Education, 80*(5), 258-260.

Contributors

Stephen J. Bagnato, Ed.D., NCSP, Office of Child Development, Early Childhood Partnerships (ECP; www.earlychildhoodpartnerships.org), University of Pittsburgh and School of Education, Department of Psychology in Education, Applied Developmental Psychology program. He is a Developmental School Psychologist and Professor of Psychology and Pediatrics at the University of Pittsburgh, Schools of Education (Applied Developmental Psychology) and Medicine (Pediatrics). He founded the Division for Early Childhood Partnerships (www.earlychildhoodpartnerships.org) at the University (Office of Child Development), and affiliated with Children's Hospital of Pittsburgh of UPMC at the LEND Center at the University as a core interdisciplinary faculty member in leadership education for Maternal and Child Health Bureau fellows specializing in neurodevelopmental disabilities. Specializing in authentic assessment and program evaluation in early childhood intervention with over 180 publications, his most recent publication is: LINKing Authentic Assessment and Early Childhood Intervention: Best Measures for Best Practices, (4th Edition), Baltimore, MD: Paul Brookes (Email: bagnatos@pitt.edu.).

Jai Wha Seo, Department of Child and Family Studies, School of Human Ecology (http://graduate.yonsei.ac.kr/en/), Yonsei University, Korea. She is a doctoral student at the Yonsei University and instructor at the Seokyeong University. Specializing in early childhood development and professional development of early childhood teachers through mentoring, she presented at international conferences and published a few articles in scientific journals (Email: jaiwha@gmail.com).

Jennifer Salaway, Office of Child Development, University of Pittsburgh. Her applied research experience involves program evaluation of early childhood programs serving at-risk youth. Dr. Salaway served as the Research Manager for the Center on Mentoring for Effective Teaching, a federally funded, applied research initiative to strengthen Head Start University partnerships through mentoring and was the primary Research Manager for the statewide evaluation of the Pennsylvania Pre-K Counts

Public Private Partnership initiative. Dr. Salaway has presented her research at both national and international conferences and has co-authored several publications focusing on improving interventions for at-risk youth. She recently co-authored a chapter in the *Oxford Handbook of School Psychology* in 2011.

Myoung Soon Kim, Department of Child and Family Studies, Yonsei University, Korea. She is a professor at the Department of Child and Family Studies, Yonsei University (http://che.yonsei.ac.kr/eng/departments/child/) and was a director of Yonsei Child Development Research Institute. Specializing in professional development for early childhood teachers, early childhood education and literacy development, and program development with publications of over 30 books and 50 research articles, she developed Korean National Childcare Curriculum and National Childcare Programs for teachers in Korea. She was acknowledged for her contribution in research, program development, and policy establishment in the field and was recognized with the Prime Minister Award. Her recent publication is *National Consulting Program Development and Research for Childcare Teachers* (2014), Seoul: Ministry of Health and Welfare (Email: kimms@yonsei.ac.kr).

Authors' Note

This research was supported by grants from the Administration for Children and Families (ACF), Office of Planning, Research and Evaluation (OPRE), U.S. Department of Health and Human Services and the Heinz Endowments. Stephen J. Bagnato and Jai Wha Seo contributed equally to this study.

Correspondence concerning this article should be addressed to Stephen J. Bagnato, University of Pittsburgh, PA; e-mail: bagnatos@pitt.edu.

The first volume of
Perspectives on Early Childhood Psychology and Education
was published in Spring 2016
by Pace University Press

Cover and Interior Design by Sara Yager
The journal was typeset in Minion and Myriad
and printed by Lightning Source in La Vergne, Tennessee

Pace University Press
Director: Sherman Raskin
Associate Director: Manuela Soares
Marketing Manager: Patricia Hinds
Design Consultant: Sara Yager

Graduate Assistants: Mary Katherine Cornfield and Angela Taldone
Student Aide: Kelsey O'Brien-Enders

www.ingramcontent.com/pod-product-compliance
Lightning Source LLC
Chambersburg PA
CBHW061445300426
44114CB00014B/1845